FOR ORGANS, PIANOS & ELECTRONIC KEYBOARDS

E-Z PLAY TODAY

79

ROADHOUSE COUNTRY

ISBN 978-1-5400-0420-8

HAL•LEONARD®

7777 W. BLUEMOUND RD. P.O. BOX 13819 MILWAUKEE, WI 53213

D0584737

E-Z Play® Today Music Notation © 1975 by HAL LEONARD LLC
E-Z PLAY and EASY ELECTRONIC KEYBOARD MUSIC are registered trademarks of HAL LEONARD LLC.

Visit Hal Leonard Online at
www.halleonard.com

Act Naturally

Registration 9
Rhythm: Country or Fox Trot

Words and Music by Vonie Morrison
and Johnny Russell

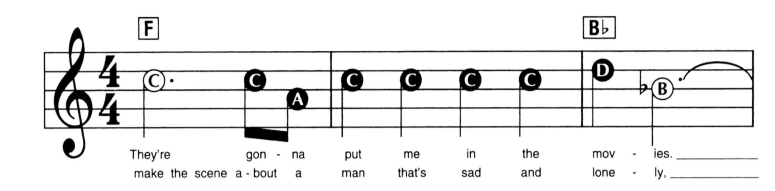

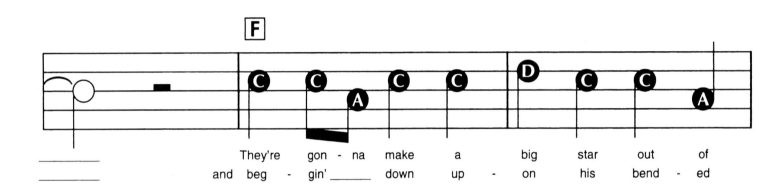

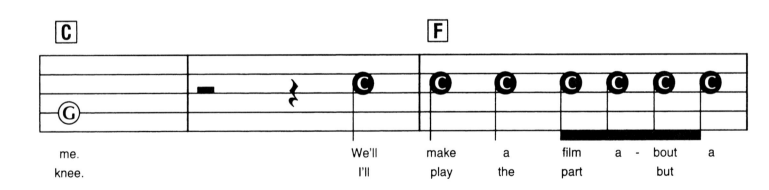

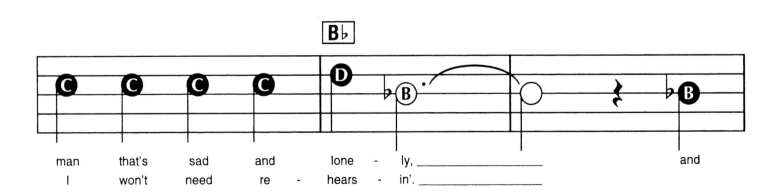

3

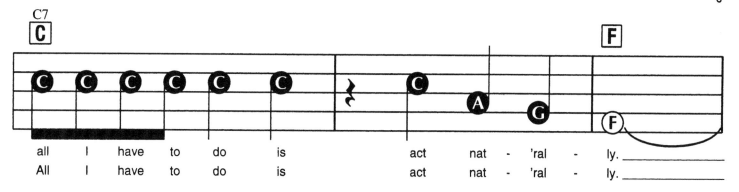

all I have to do is act nat - 'ral - ly. _____
All I have to do is act nat - 'ral - ly. _____

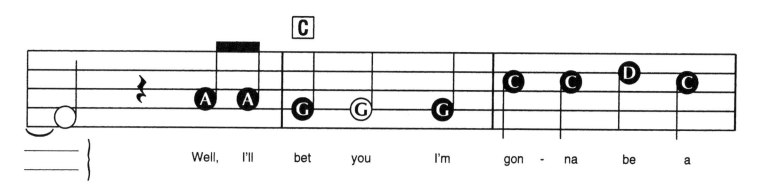

_____ Well, I'll bet you I'm gon - na be a

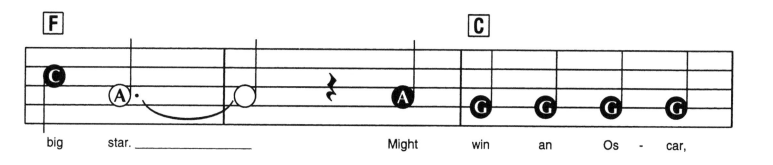

big star. _____ Might win an Os - car,

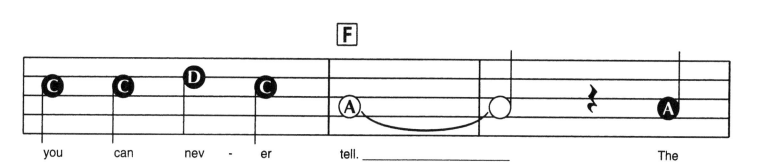

you can nev - er tell. _____ The

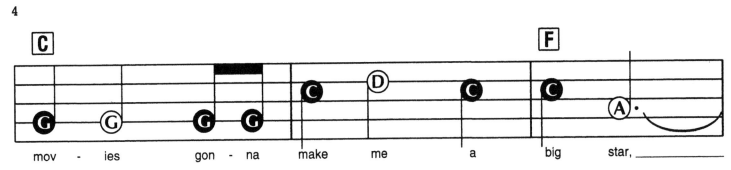

mov - ies gon - na make me a big star, _____

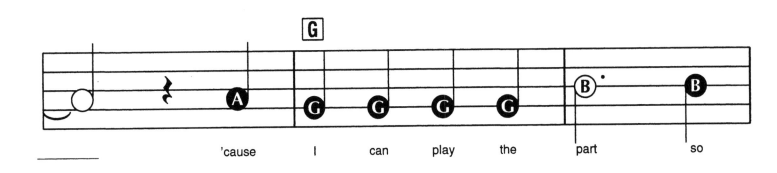

_____ 'cause I can play the part so

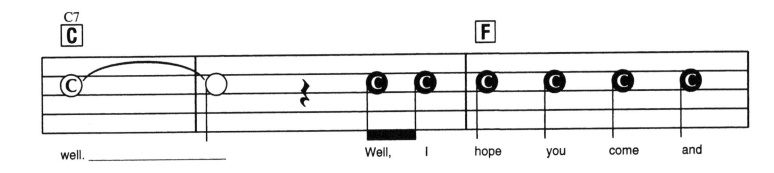

well. _____ Well, I hope you come and

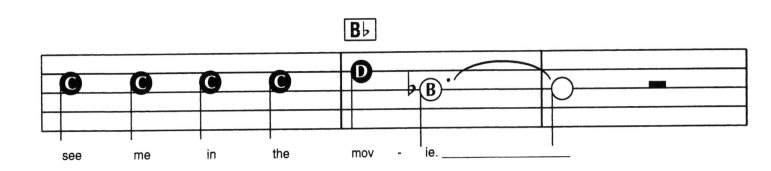

see me in the mov - ie. _____

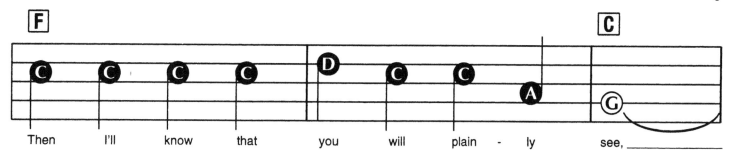

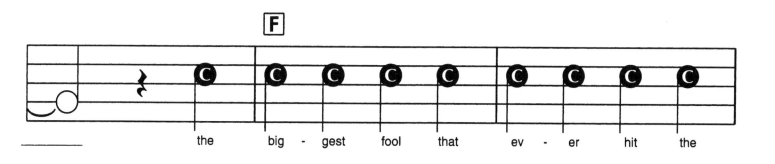

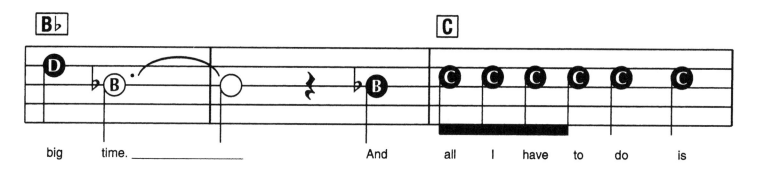

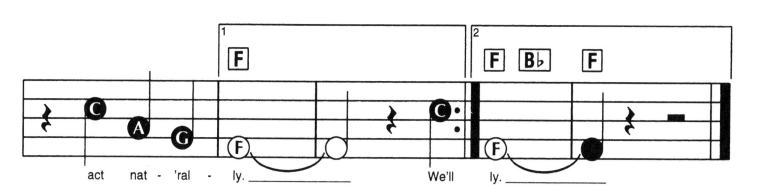

All My Ex's Live in Texas

Registration 4
Rhythm: Country or Shuffle

Words and Music by Lyndia J. Shafer
and Sanger D. Shafer

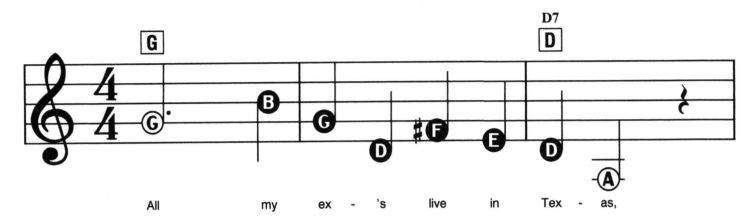

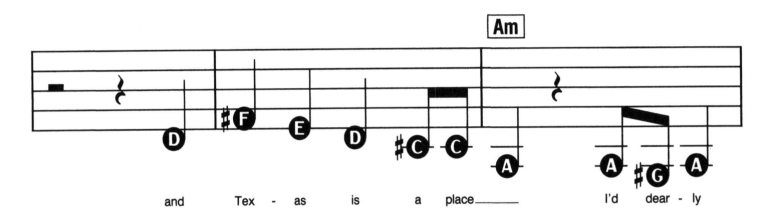

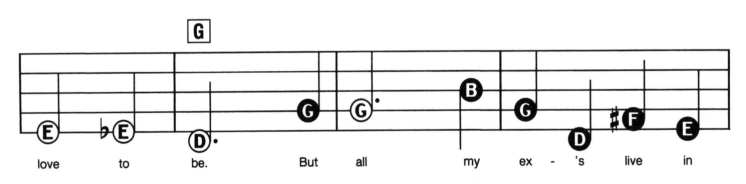

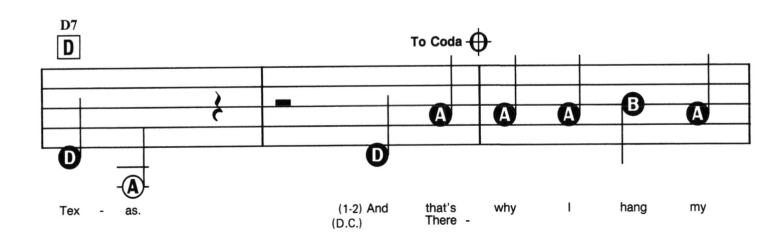

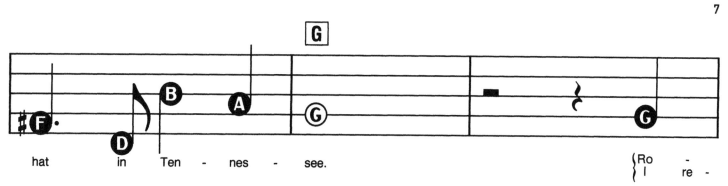

hat in Ten - nes - see. {Ro - {I re -

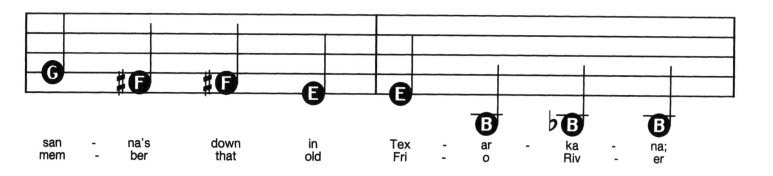

san - na's down in Tex - ar - ka - na;
mem - ber that old Fri - o Riv - er

Am

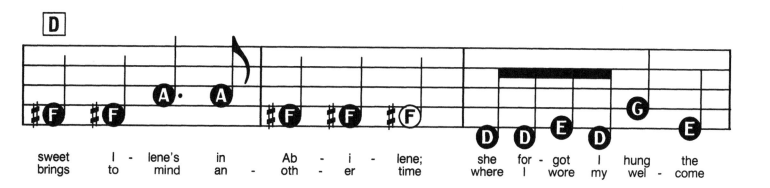

want - ed me to push her broom. And
where I learned to swim. And it

D

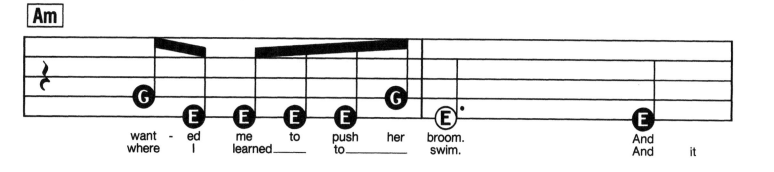

sweet I - lene's in Ab - i - lene; she for - got I hung the
brings to mind an - oth - er time where I wore my wel - come

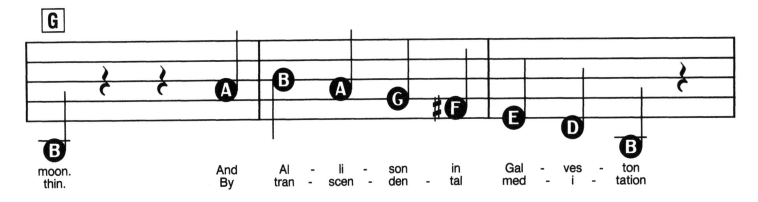

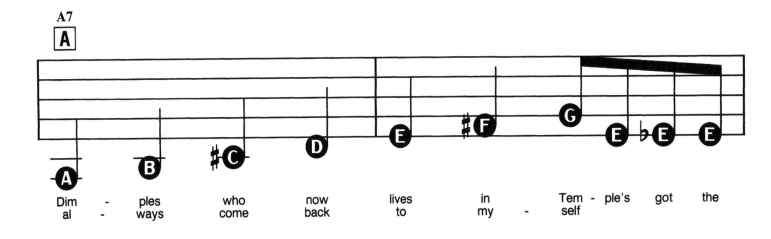

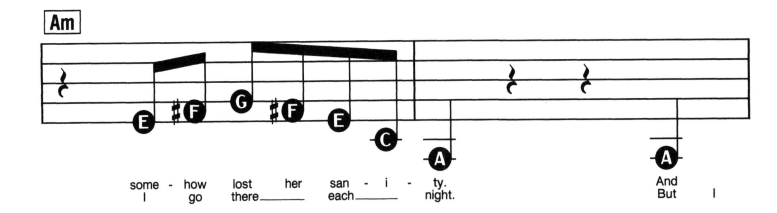

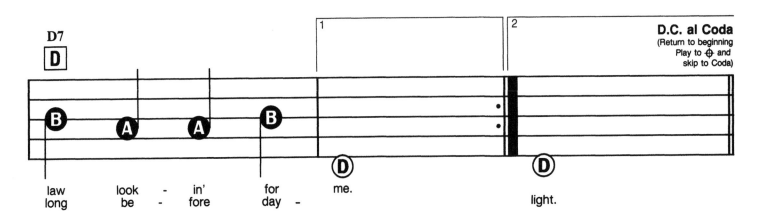

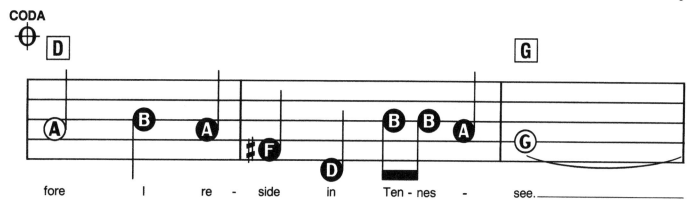

fore   I   re - side   in   Ten - nes -   see. _____

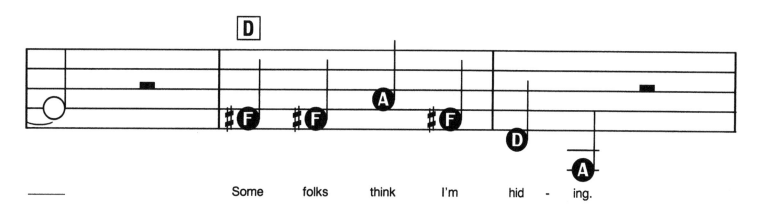

_____   Some   folks   think   I'm   hid - ing.

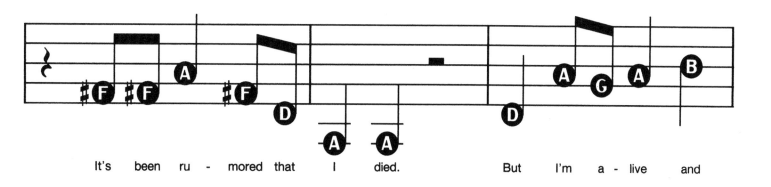

It's   been   ru - mored   that   I   died.   But   I'm   a - live   and

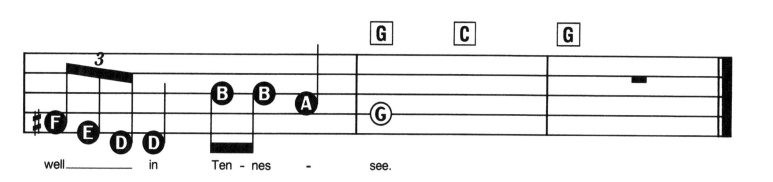

well _____   in   Ten - nes -   see.

Coal Miner's Daughter

Registration 8
Rhythm: Country or Fox Trot

Words and Music by
Loretta Lynn

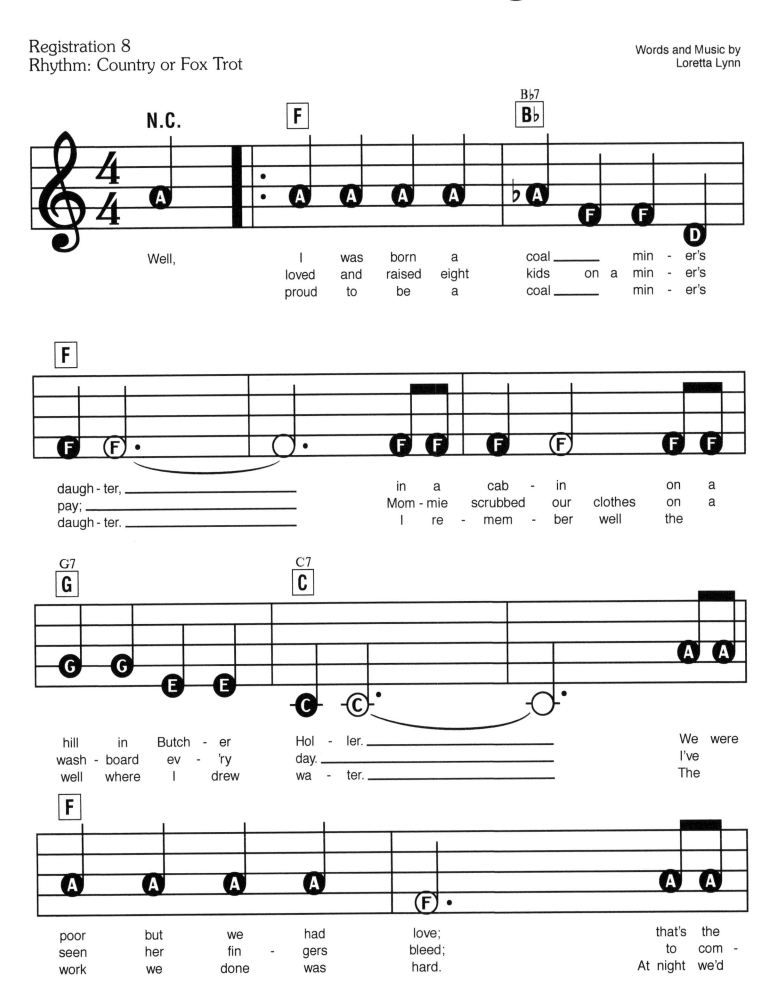

Convoy

Registration 4
Rhythm: Country Swing or Bluegrass

Words and Music by William D. Fries
and Chip Davis

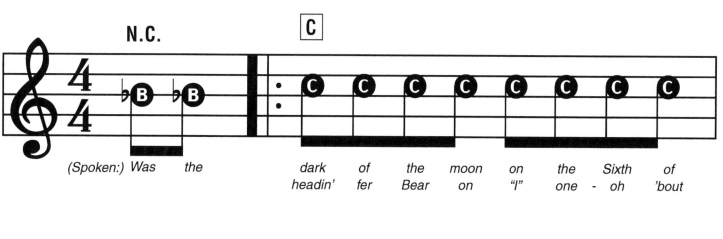

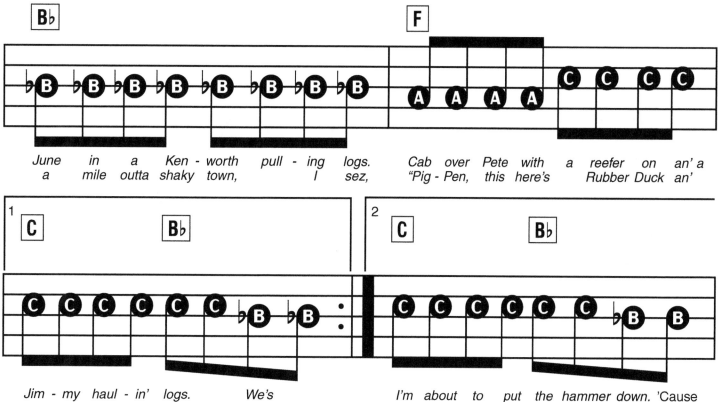

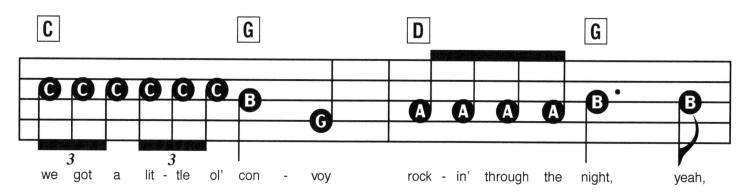

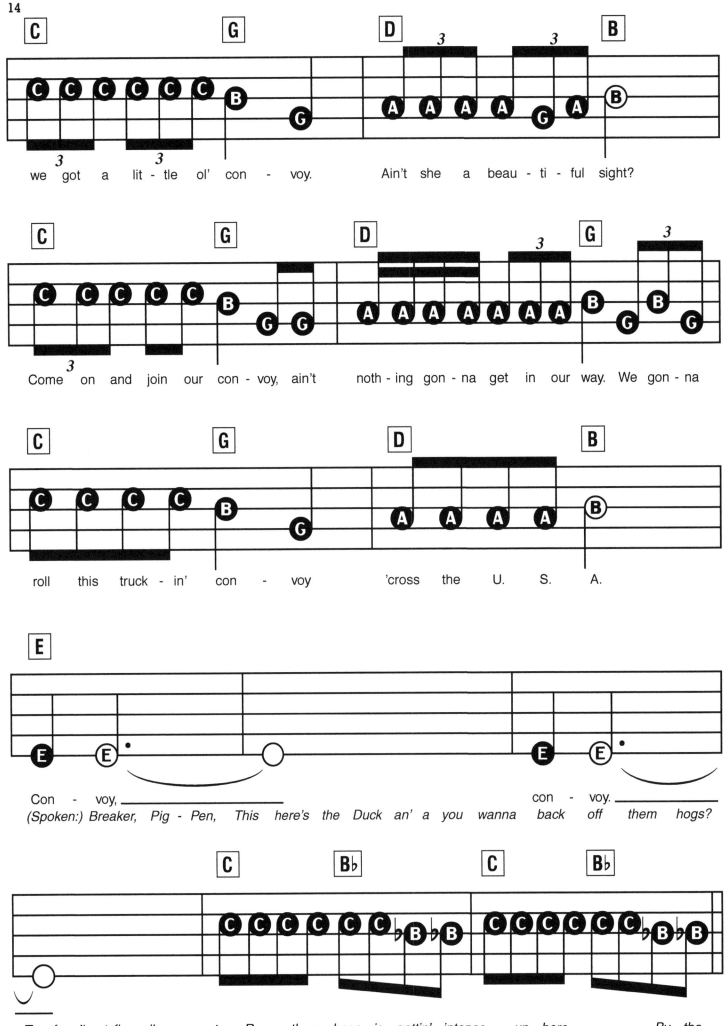

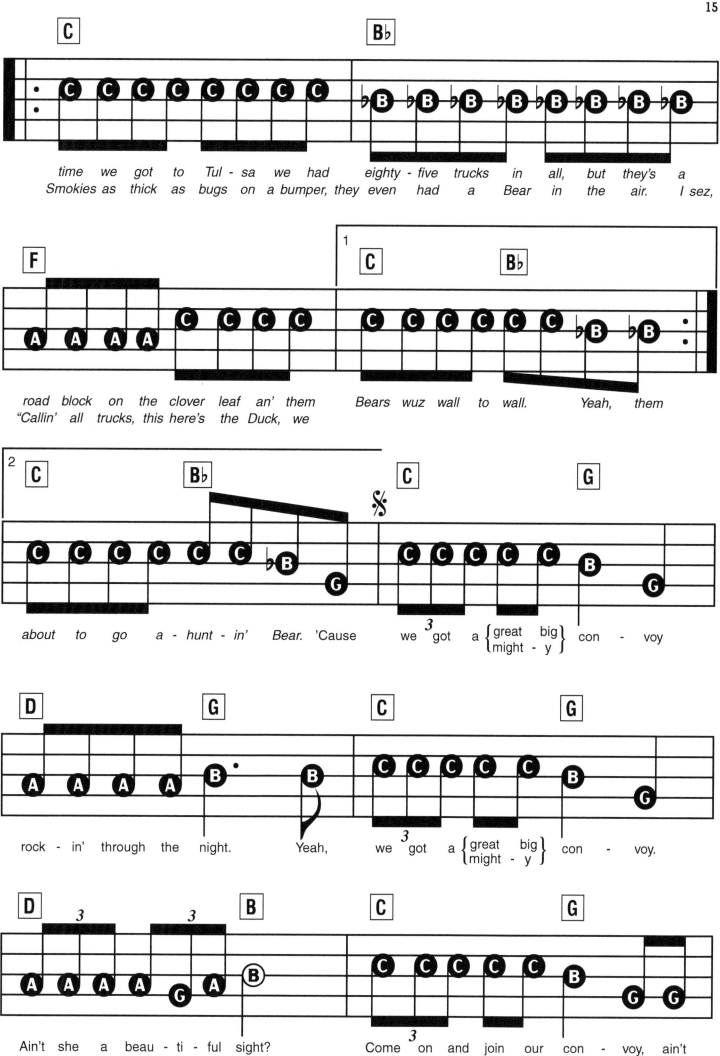

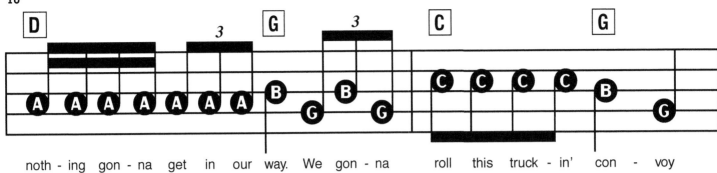

noth - ing gon - na get in our way. We gon - na roll this truck - in' con - voy

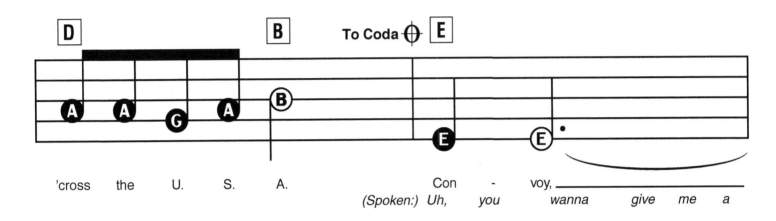

'cross the U. S. A. Con - voy, _____
(Spoken:) Uh, you wanna give me a

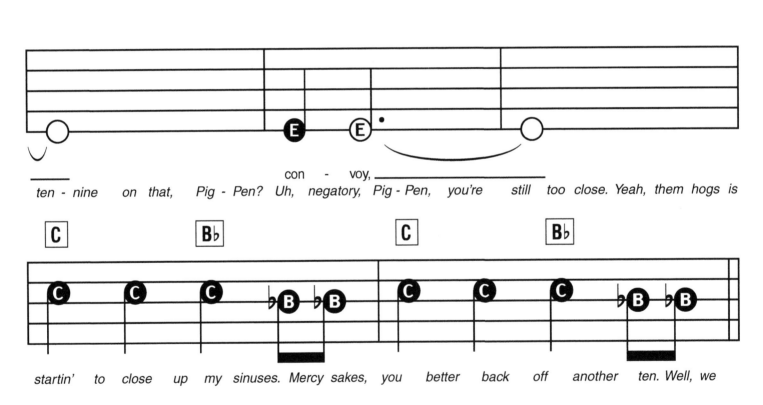

_____ con - voy, _____
ten - nine on that, Pig - Pen? Uh, negatory, Pig - Pen, you're still too close. Yeah, them hogs is

startin' to close up my sinuses. Mercy sakes, you better back off another ten. Well, we

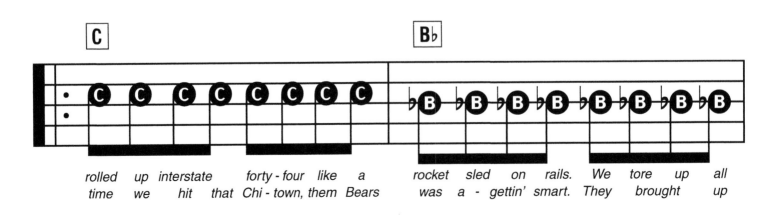

rolled up interstate forty - four like a rocket sled on rails. We tore up all
time we hit that Chi - town, them Bears was a - gettin' smart. They brought up

17

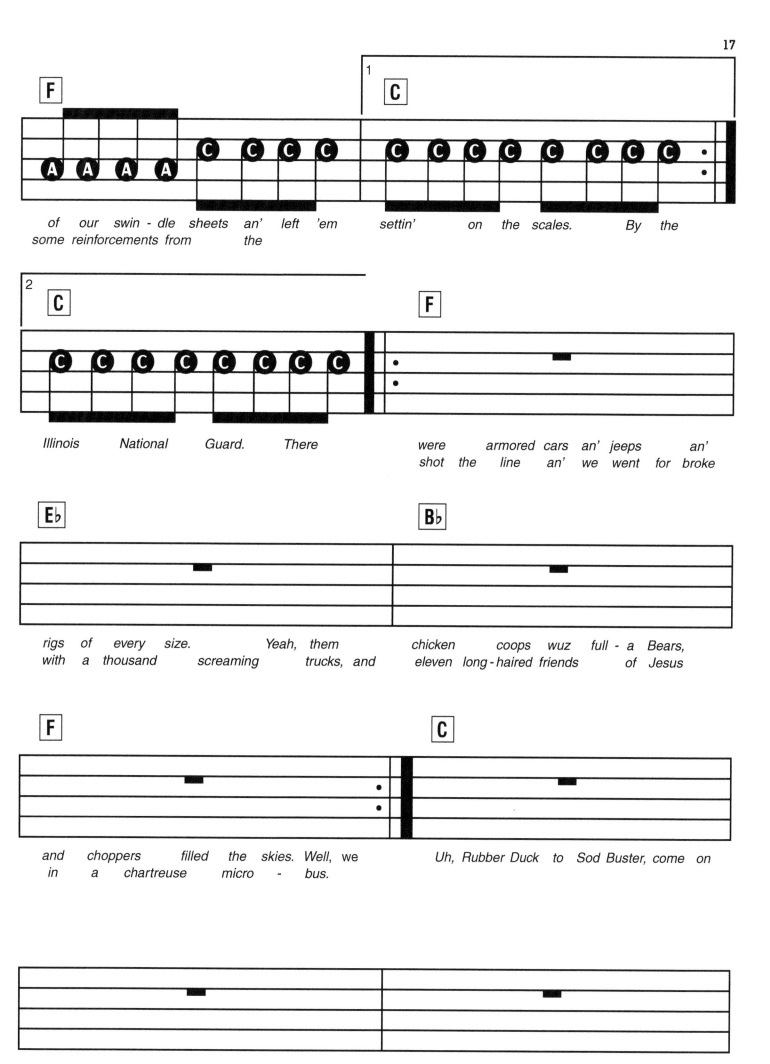

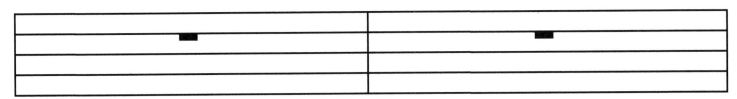

that suicide jockey? Yeah he's haulin' dynamite an' he needs all the help he

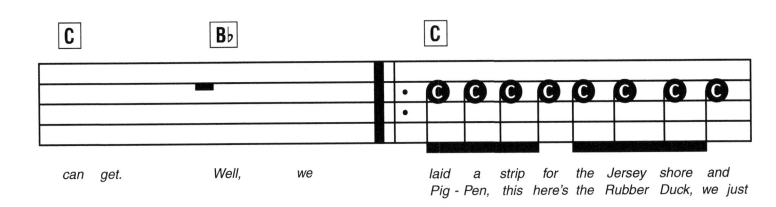

can get. Well, we

laid a strip for the Jersey shore and
Pig - Pen, this here's the Rubber Duck, we just

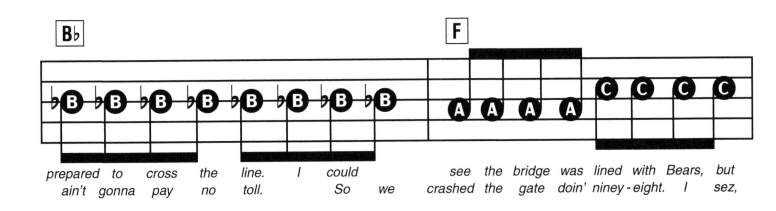

prepared to cross the line. I could
ain't gonna pay no toll. So we

see the bridge was lined with Bears, but
crashed the gate doin' niney - eight. I sez,

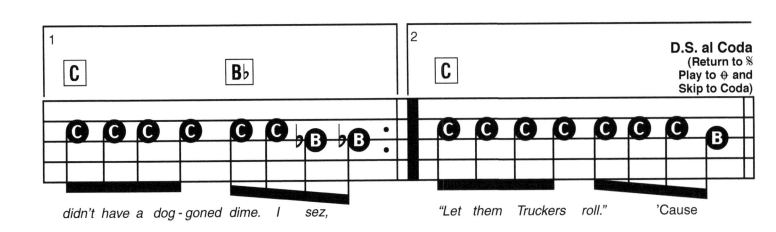

D.S. al Coda
(Return to %
Play to ⊕ and
Skip to Coda)

didn't have a dog - goned dime. I sez,

"Let them Truckers roll." 'Cause

CODA

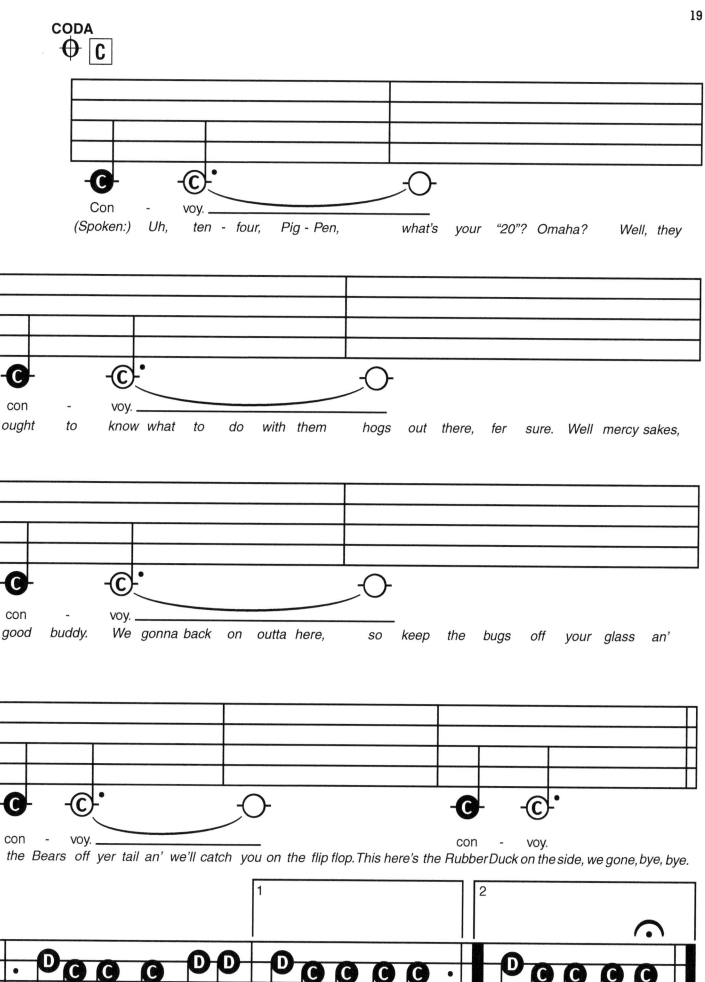

Con - voy. _____
(Spoken:) Uh,   ten - four,   Pig - Pen,   what's   your   "20"? Omaha?   Well,   they

con - voy. _____
ought   to   know what   to   do   with   them   hogs   out   there,   fer   sure. Well mercy sakes,

con - voy. _____
good   buddy.   We gonna back   on   outta here,   so   keep   the   bugs   off   your   glass   an'

con - voy. _____   con - voy.
the Bears off yer tail an' we'll catch you on the flip flop. This here's the Rubber Duck on the side, we gone, bye, bye.

(Instrumental)

Drinkin' Thing

Registration 4
Rhythm: Country or Fox Trot

Words and Music by
Wayne Carson Thompson

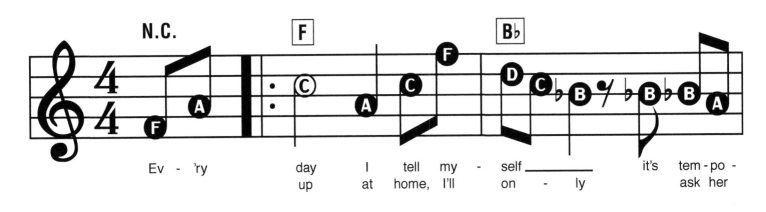

Ev - 'ry day I tell my - self _____ it's tem - po -
up at home, I'll on - ly ask her

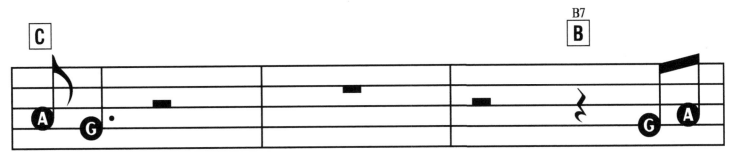

rar - y, that it's
ques - tions. She'd

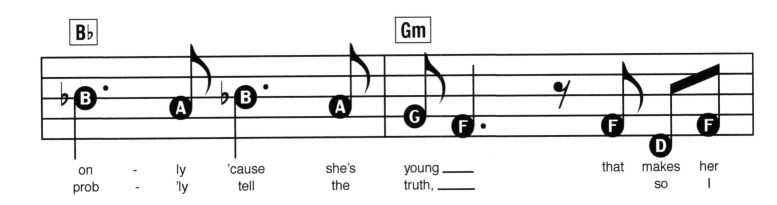

on - ly 'cause she's young _____ that makes her
prob - 'ly tell the truth, _____ so I

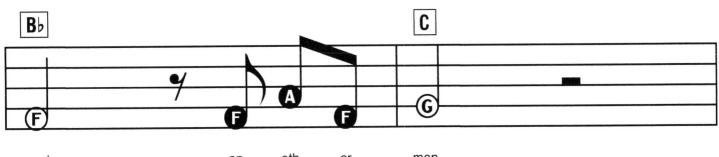

want an - oth - er man.
don't e - ven ask.

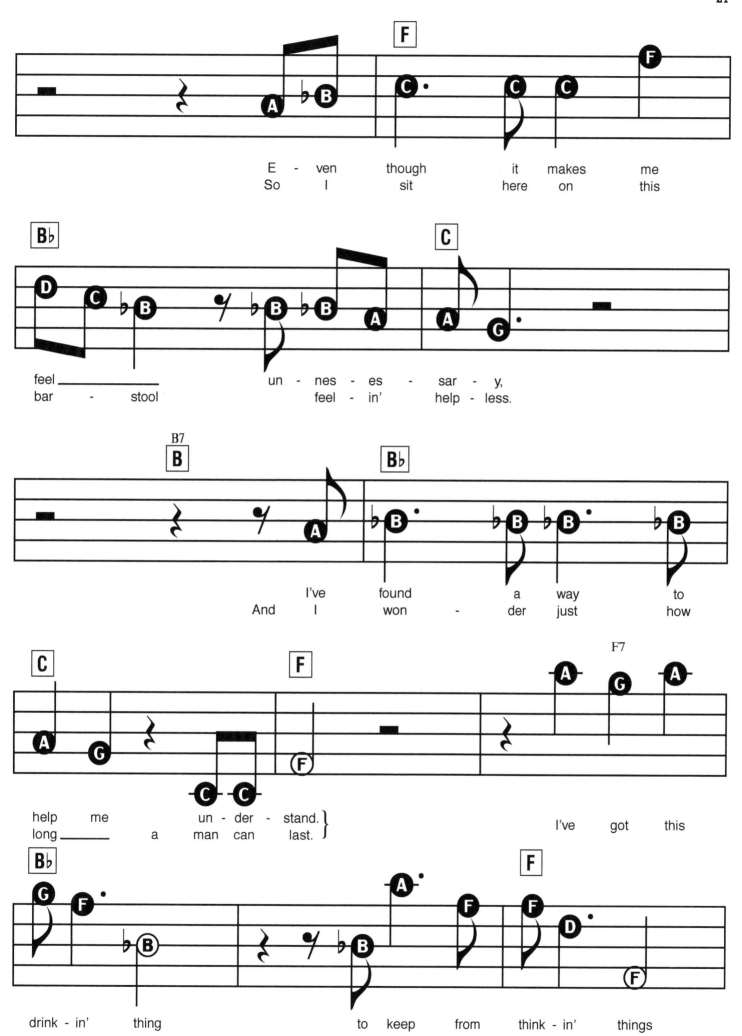

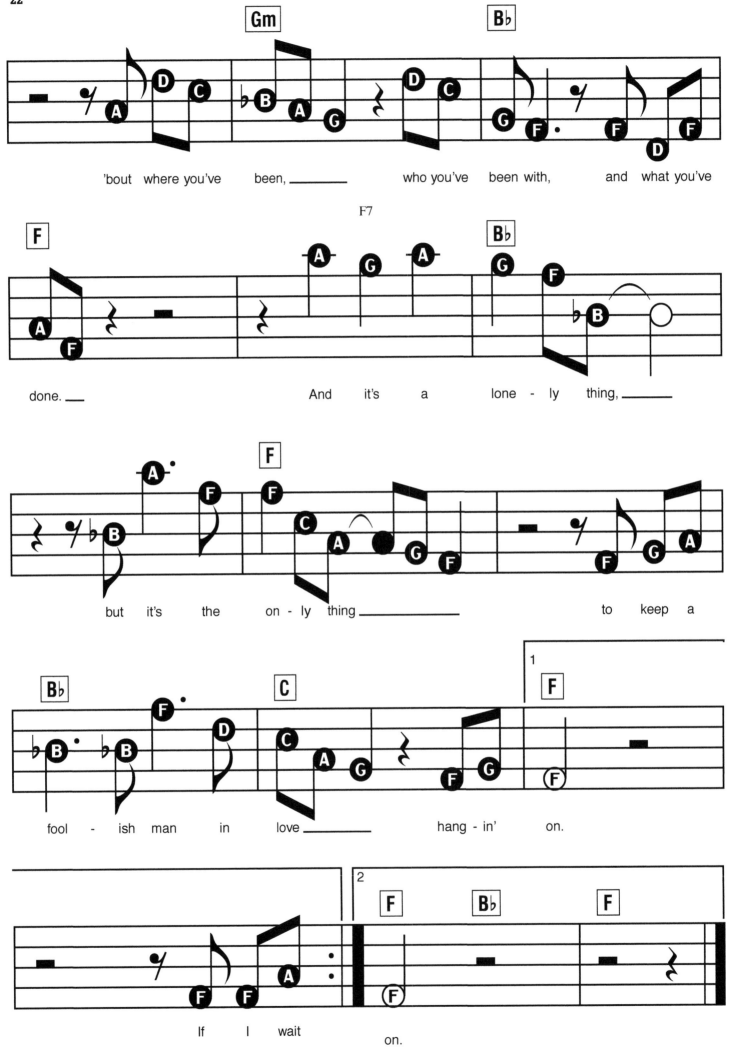

El Paso

Registration 5
Rhythm: Waltz

Words and Music by
Marty Robbins

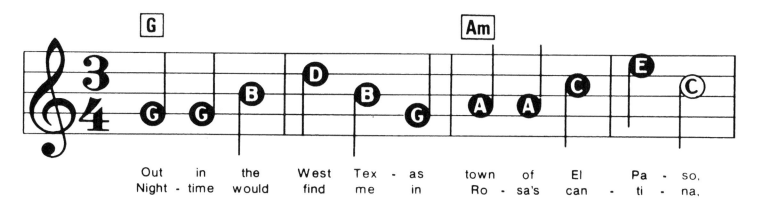

Out in the West Tex - as town of El Pa - so,
Night - time would find me in Ro - sa's can - ti - na,

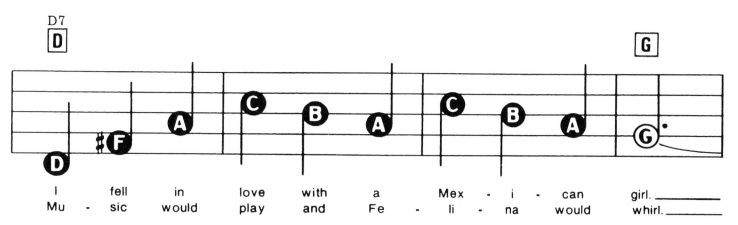

I fell in love with a Mex - i - can girl. _____
Mu - sic would play and a Fe - li - na would whirl. _____

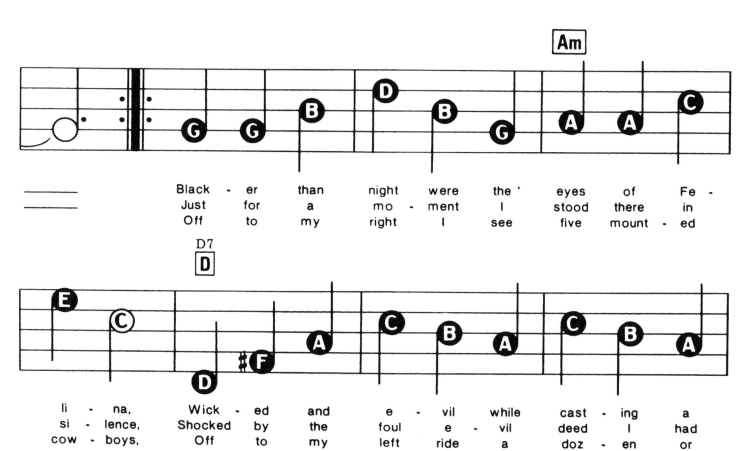

_____ Black - er than night were the eyes of Fe -
_____ Just for a mo - ment I stood there in
Off to my right I see five mount - ed

li - na, Wick - ed and e - vil while cast - ing a
si - lence, Shocked by the foul e - vil deed I had
cow - boys, Off to my left ride a doz - en or

24

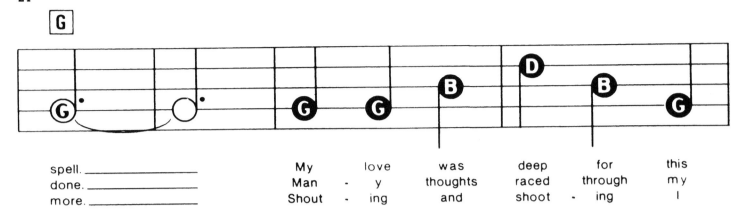

spell. _____
done. _____
more. _____

My love was deep for this
Man - y thoughts raced through my
Shout - ing and shoot - ing I

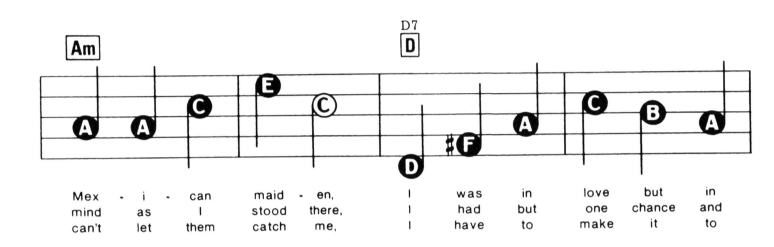

Mex - i - can maid - en, I was in love but in
mind as I stood there, I had but to one chance and
can't let them catch me, I have to make it to

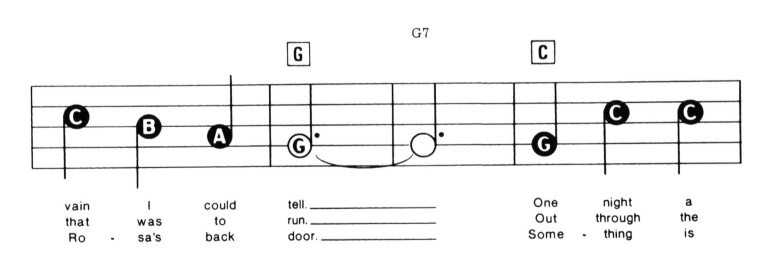

vain I could tell. _____
that was to run. _____
Ro - sa's back door. _____

One night a
Out through the
Some - thing is

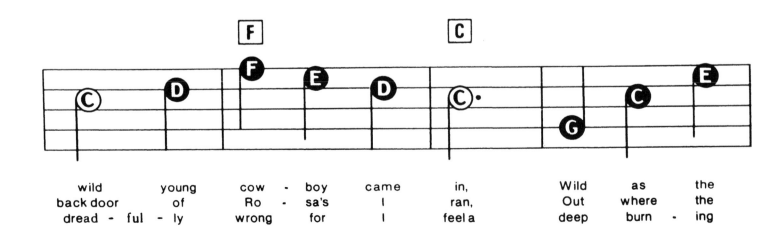

wild young cow - boy came in,
back door of Ro - sa's I ran,
dread - ful - ly wrong for I feel a

Wild as the
Out where the
Out deep burn - ing

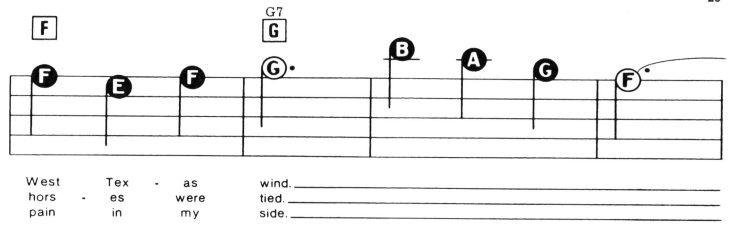

West   Tex - as   wind. _____
hors - es   were   tied. _____
pain   in   my   side. _____

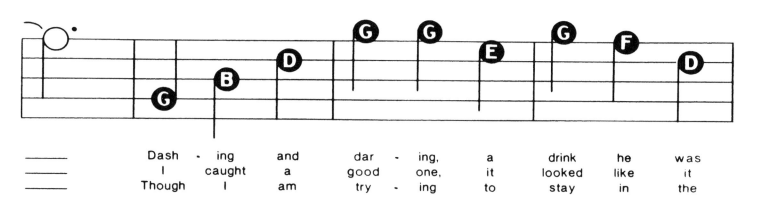

_____ Dash - ing and   dar - ing, a   drink   he   was
_____ I   caught a   good   one, it   looked   like   it
_____ Though I   am   try - ing to   stay   in   the

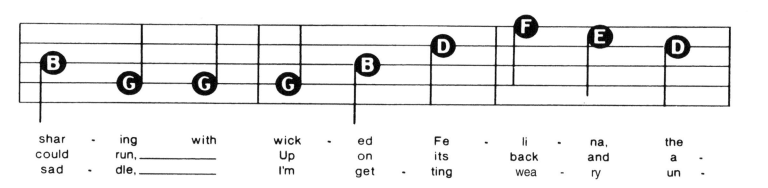

shar - ing   with   wick - ed   Fe - li - na, the
could   run,_____ Up   on   its   back   and   a -
sad - dle,_____ I'm   get - ting wea - ry   un -

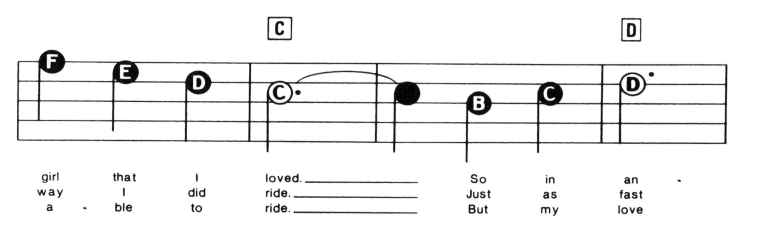

girl   that   I   loved._____ So   in   an -
way   I   did   ride._____ Just   as   fast
a - ble   to   ride._____ But   my   love

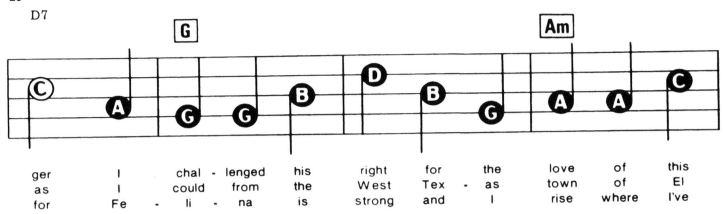

ger   I   chal - lenged his   right   for   the   love   of   this
as   I   could from   the   West Tex - as   town   of   El
for   Fe - li - na   is   strong and   I   rise where I've

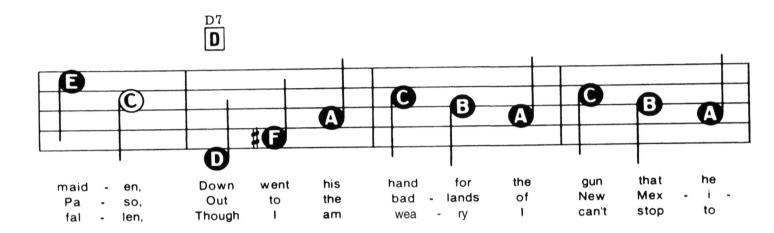

maid - en,   Down went his   hand   for   the   gun   that he
Pa - so,   Out to the   bad - lands of   New Mex - i -
fal - len, Though I am wea - ry I   can't stop to

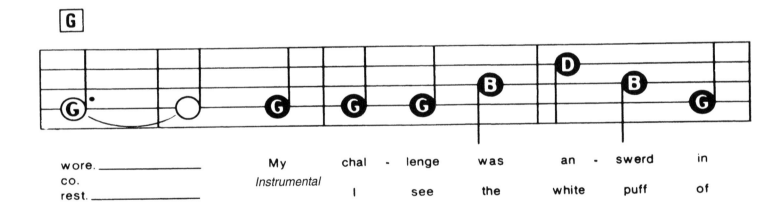

wore._____   My chal - lenge was   an - swerd in
co._____   *Instrumental*   I   see the white puff of
rest._____

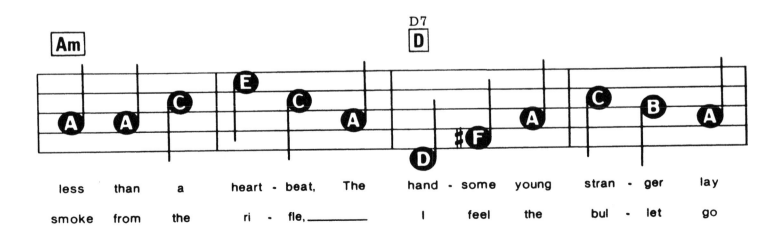

less than a   heart - beat, The hand - some young stran - ger lay
smoke from the ri - fle,_____   I   feel the bul - let go

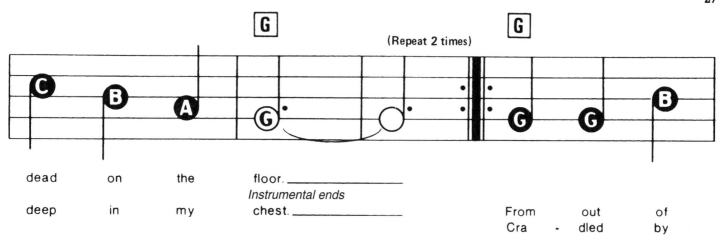

dead   on   the   floor._____
Instrumental ends
deep   in   my   chest._____

From   out   of
Cra - dled   by

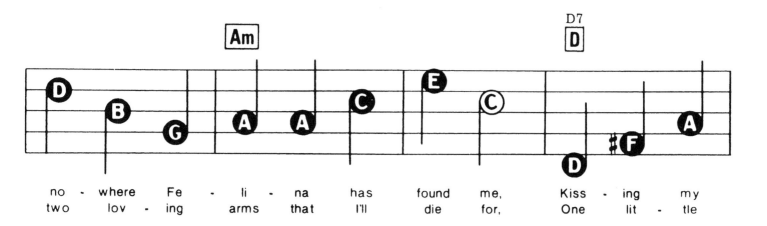

no - where   Fe - li - na   has   found   me,   Kiss - ing   my
two lov - ing   arms that I'll   die   for,   One   lit - tle

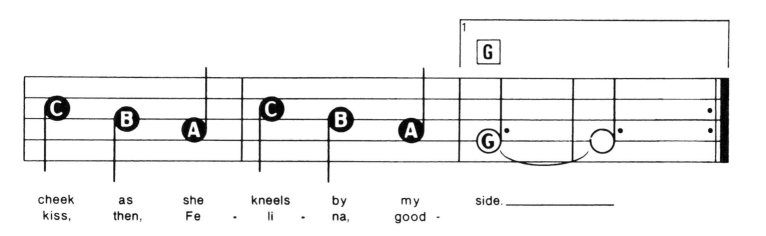

cheek   as   she   kneels   by   my   side._____
kiss, then, Fe - li - na, good -

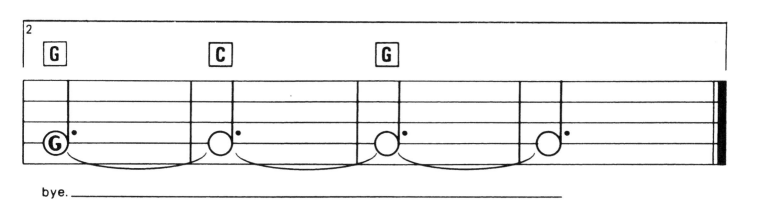

bye._____

Folsom Prison Blues

Registration 3
Rhythm: Rock or Fox Trot

Words and Music by
John R. Cash

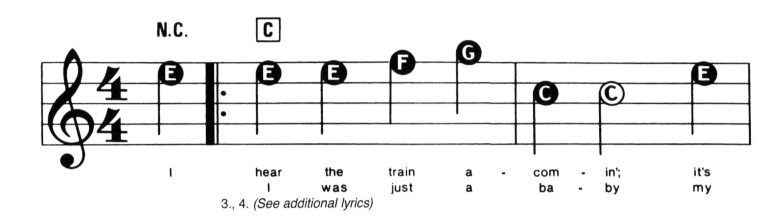

3., 4. *(See additional lyrics)*

I   hear   the   train   a -   com -   in';   it's
I   was   just   a   ba -   by   my

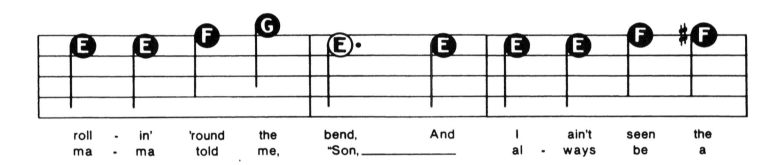

roll - in'   'round   the   bend,   And   I   ain't   seen   the
ma - ma   told   me,   "Son,_____   al - ways   be   a

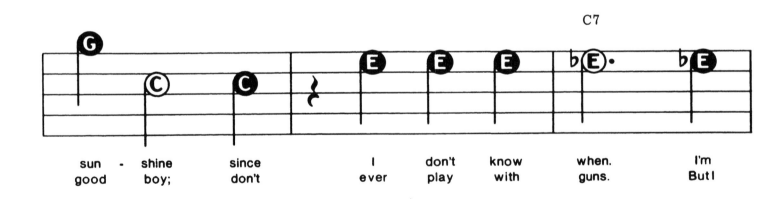

sun - shine   since   I   don't   know   when.   I'm
good   boy;   don't   ever   play   with   guns.   But I

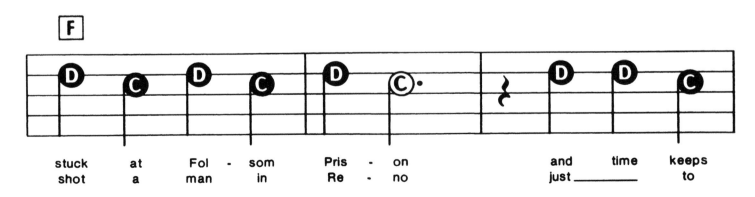

stuck   at   Fol - som   Pris - on   and   time   keeps
shot   a   man   in   Re - no   just_____   to

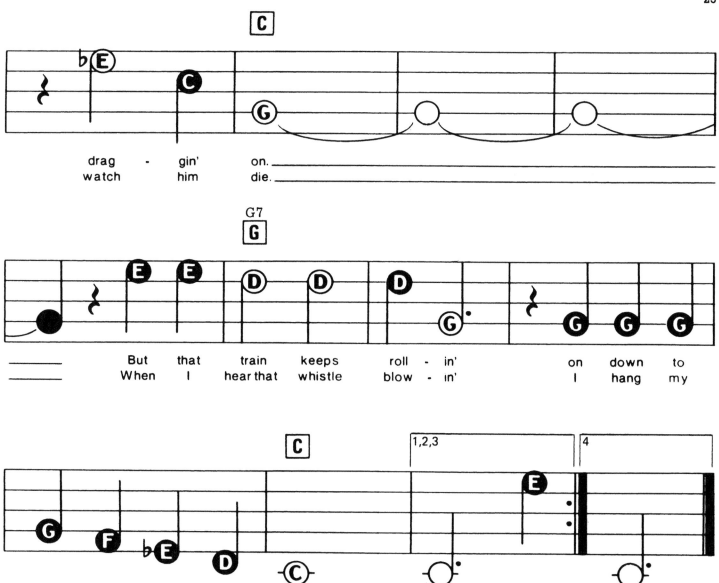

Additional Lyrics

3. I bet there's rich folks eatin' in a fancy dining car.
   They're prob'ly drinkin' coffee and smokin' big cigars,
   But I know I had it comin', I know I can't be free,
   But those people keep a-movin', and that's what tortures me.

4. Well, if they freed me from this prison, if that railroad train was mine,
   I bet I'd move over a little farther down the line,
   Far from Folsom Prison, that's where I want to stay.
   And I'd let that lonesome whistle blow my blues away.

Friends in Low Places

Registration 1
Rhythm: Swing or Country

Words and Music by DeWayne Blackwell
and Earl Bud Lee

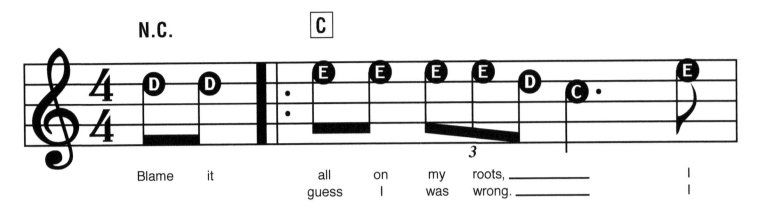

Blame it all on my roots, ____ I
guess I was wrong. ____ I

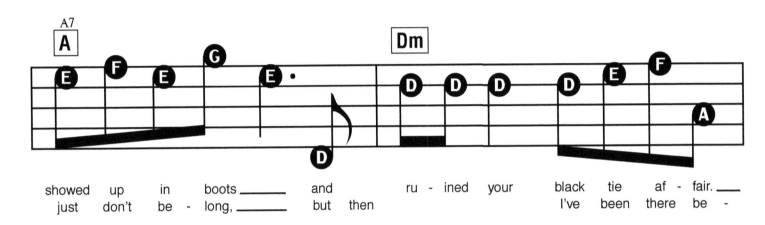

showed up in boots ____ and then ru - ined your black tie af - fair. ____
just don't be - long, ____ but then I've been there be -

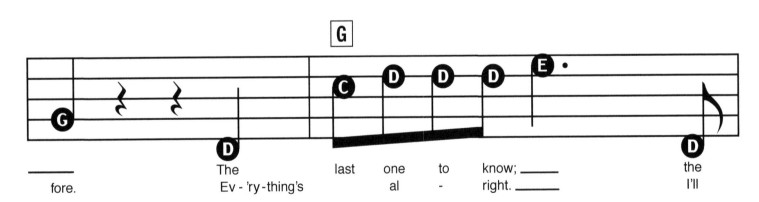

fore. The last one to know; ____ the
Ev - 'ry-thing's al - right. ____ I'll

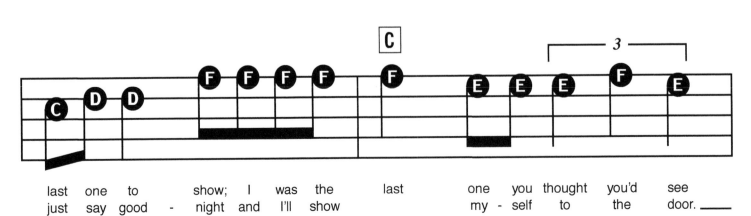

last one to show; I was the last one you thought you'd see
just say good - night and I'll show my - self to the door. ____

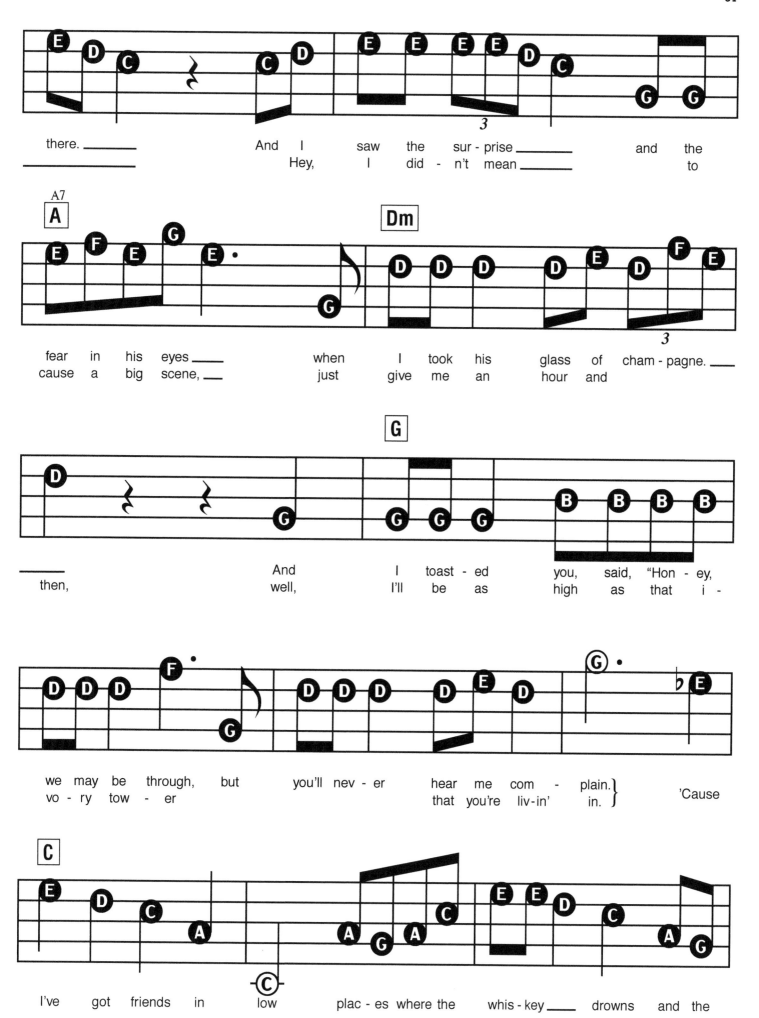

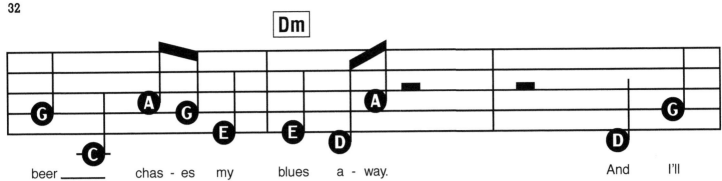

beer _____ chas - es my blues a - way. And I'll

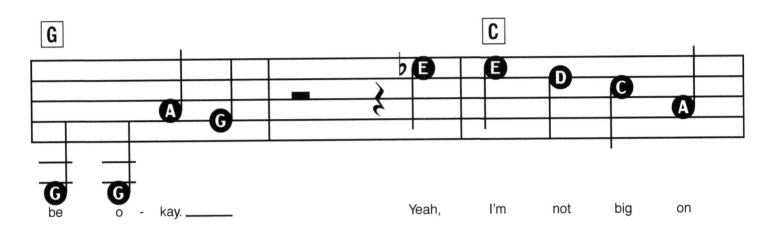

be o - kay. _____ Yeah, I'm not big on

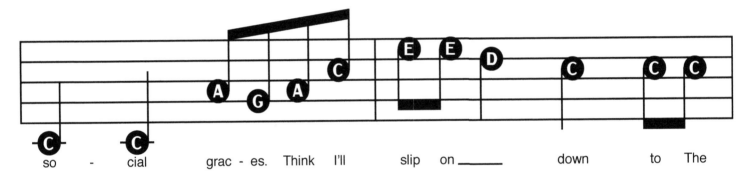

so - cial grac - es. Think I'll slip on _____ down to The

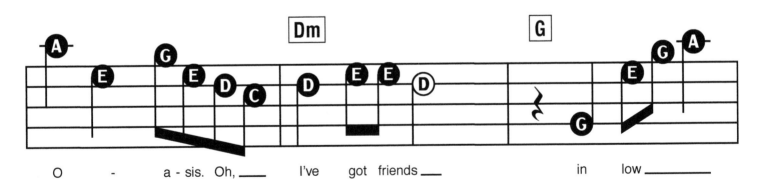

O - a - sis. Oh, ___ I've got friends ___ in low _____

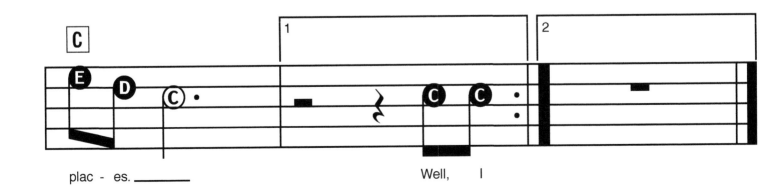

plac - es. _____ Well, I

Honky Tonk Heroes

Registration 4
Rhythm: Country Swing

Words and Music by
Billy Joe Shaver

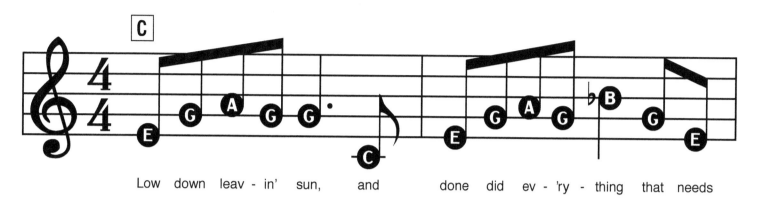

Low down leav - in' sun, and done did ev - 'ry - thing that needs

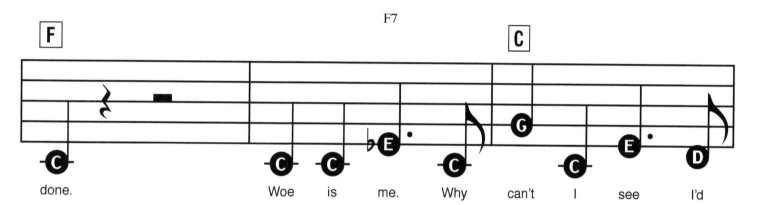

done. Woe is me. Why can't I see I'd

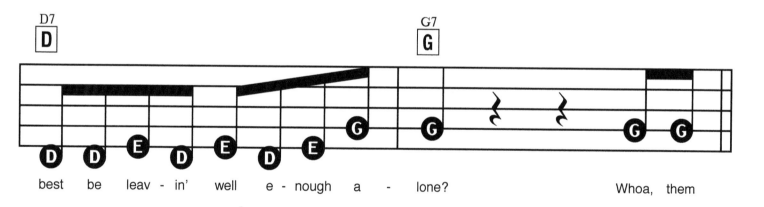

best be leav - in' well e - nough a - lone? Whoa, them

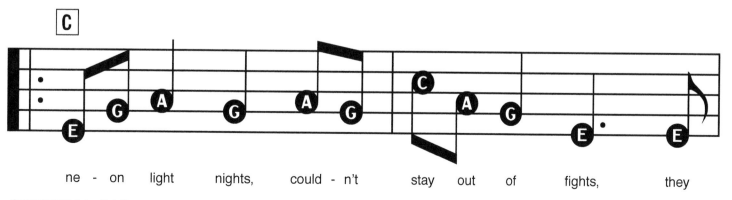

ne - on light nights, could - n't stay out of fights, they

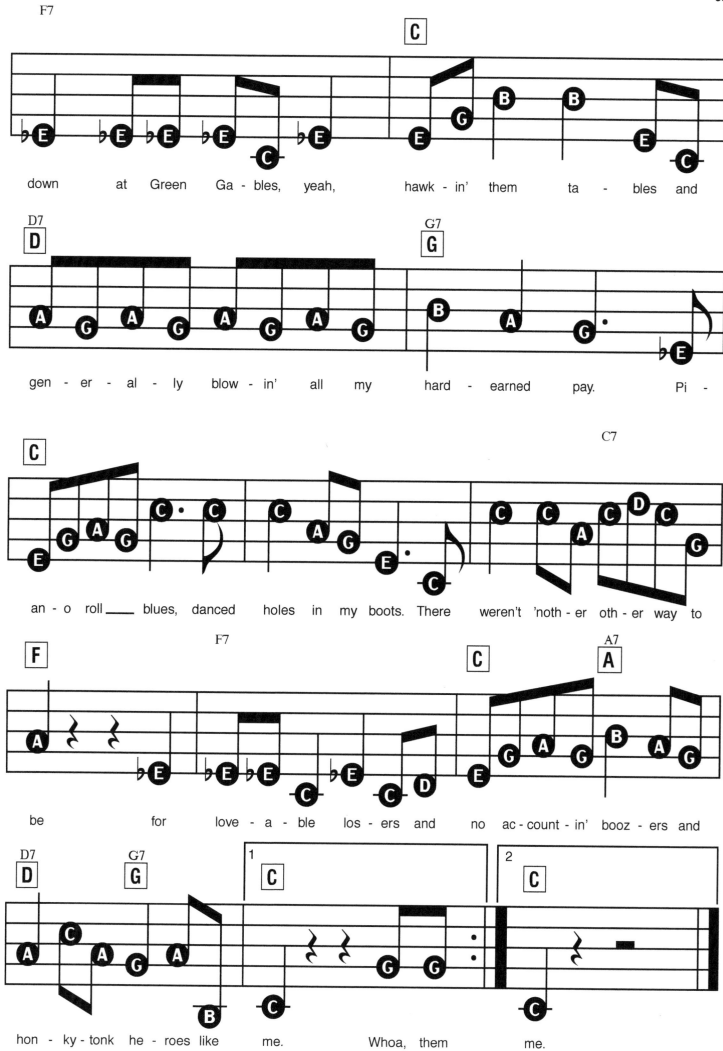

A Good Hearted Woman

Registration 4
Rhythm: Country

Words and Music by Willie Nelson
and Waylon Jennings

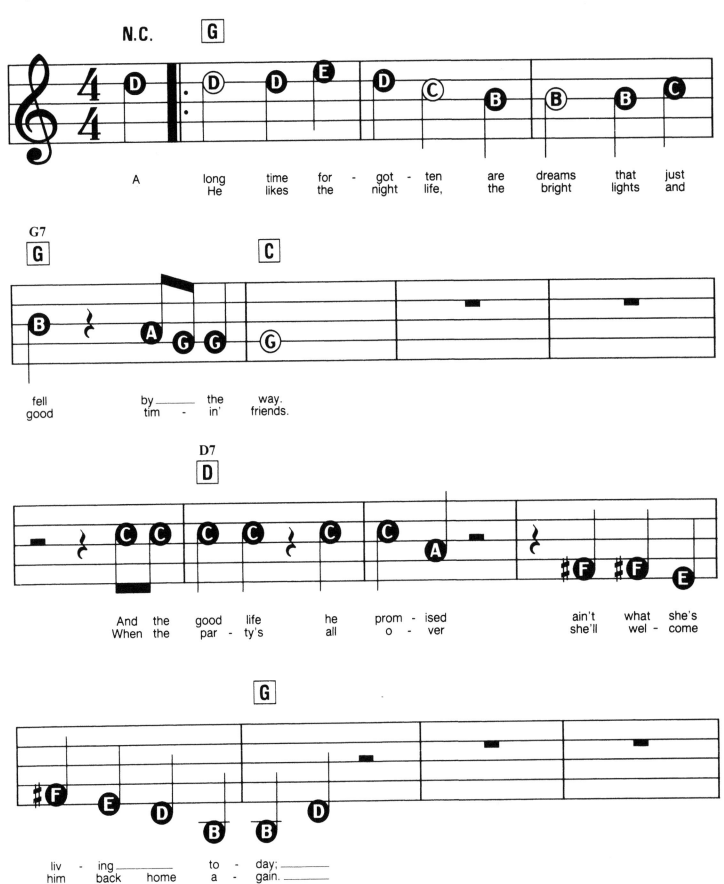

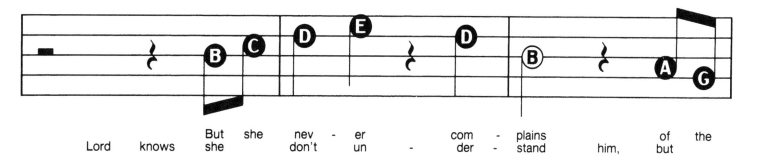

Lord knows But she nev - er com - plains of the

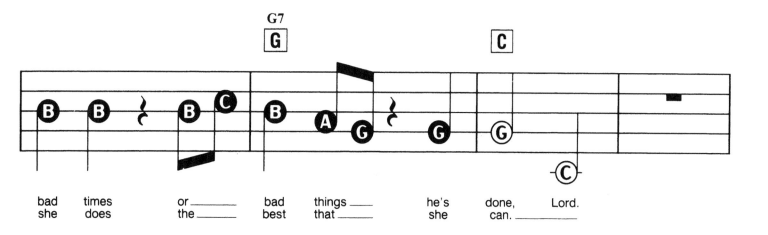

bad times or _____ bad things _____ he's done, Lord.
she does the _____ best that _____ she can. _____

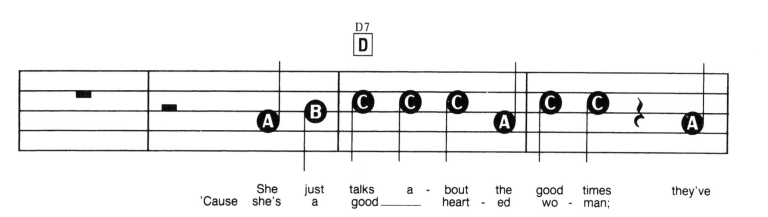

'Cause She just talks a - bout the good times they've
She's a good _____ heart - ed wo - man;

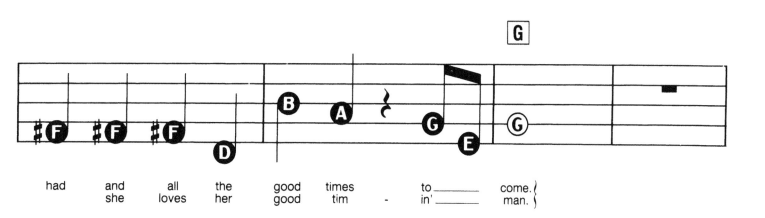

had and all the good times to _____ come.
she loves her good tim - in' _____ man.

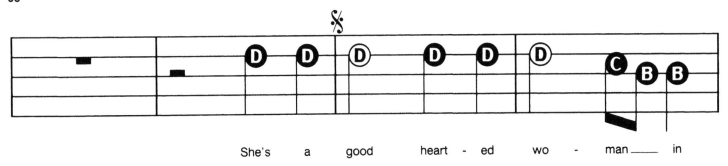

She's a good heart - ed wo - man ___ in

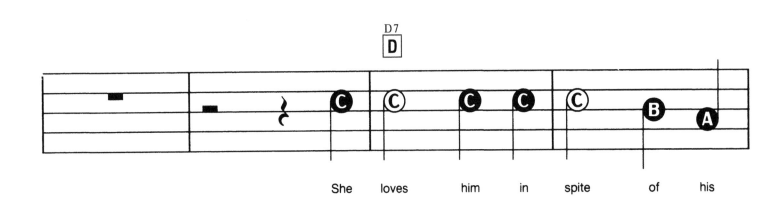

love with a good tim - in' man.

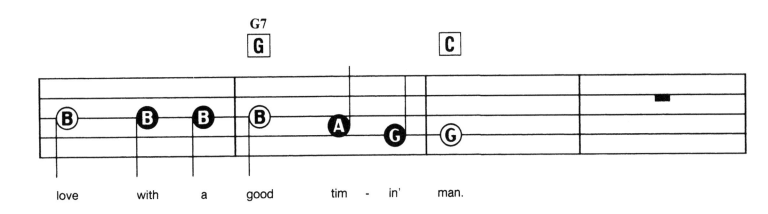

She loves him in spite of his

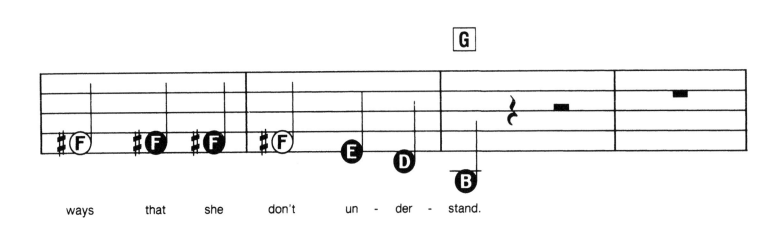

ways that she don't un - der - stand.

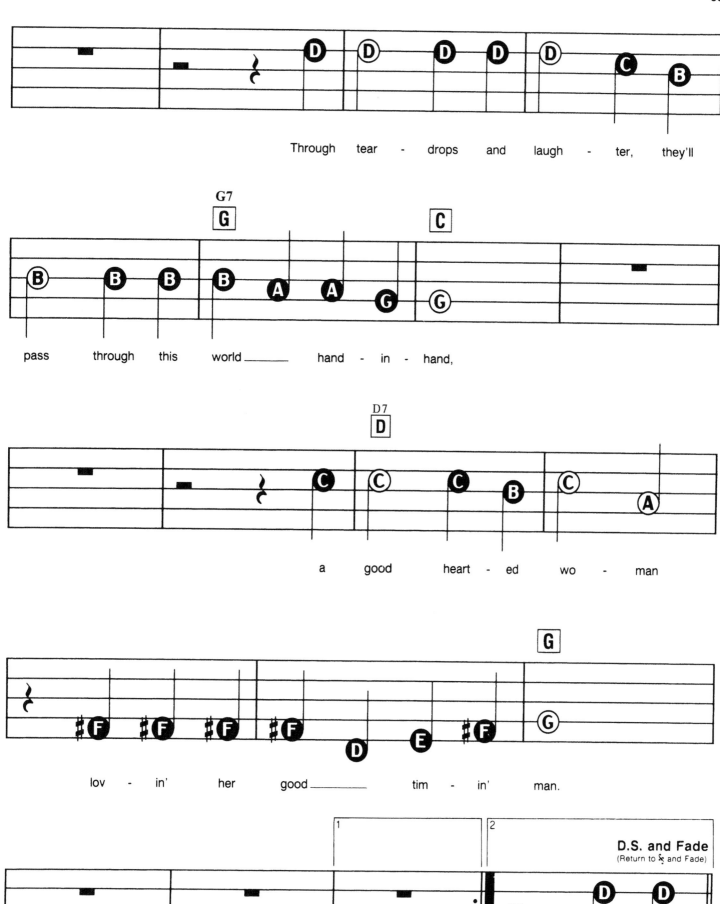

Through   tear - drops   and   laugh - ter,   they'll

pass   through   this   world _____ hand - in - hand,

a   good   heart - ed   wo - man

lov - in'   her   good _____ tim - in'   man.

D.S. and Fade
(Return to 𝄋 and Fade)

She's   a

Guitars, Cadillacs

Registration 7
Rhythm: Shuffle or Swing

Words and Music by
Dwight Yoakam

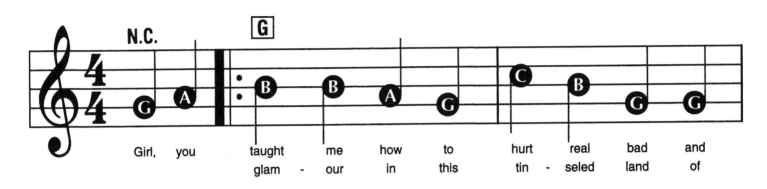

Girl, you taught me how to hurt real bad and
glam - our in this tin - seled land of

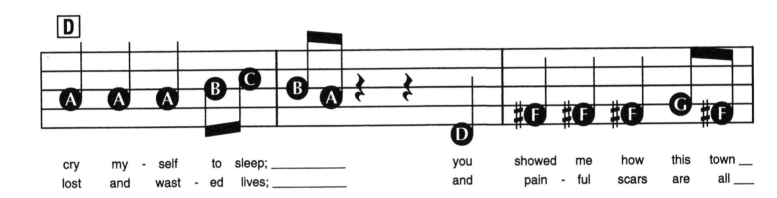

cry my - self to sleep; _____ you showed me how this town __
lost and wast - ed lives; _____ and pain - ful scars are all __

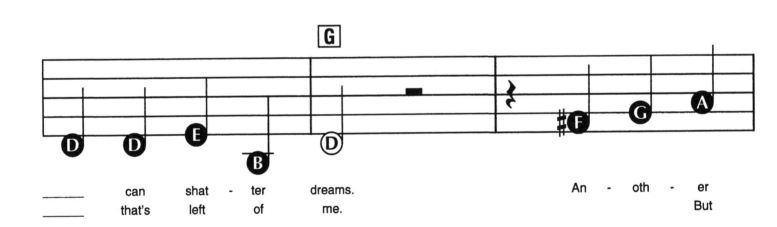

_____ can shat - ter dreams. An - oth - er
_____ that's left of me. But

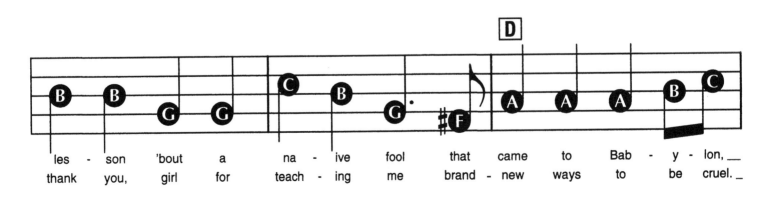

les - son 'bout a na - ive fool that came to Bab - y - lon, __
thank you, girl for teach - ing me brand - new ways to be cruel. _

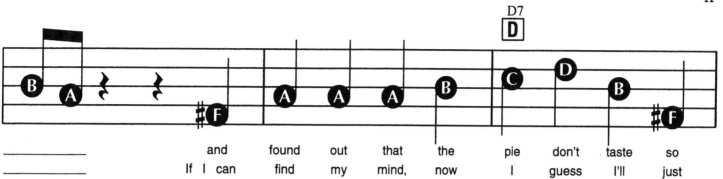

and found out that the pie don't taste so
If I can find my mind, now I guess I'll just

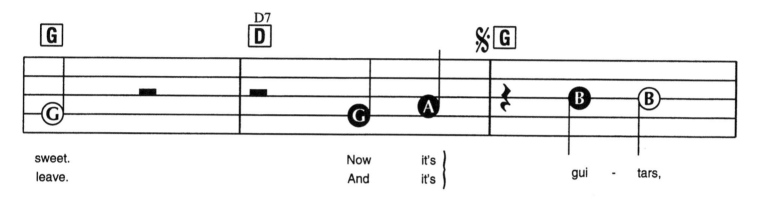

sweet.
leave.
Now it's
And it's
gui - tars,

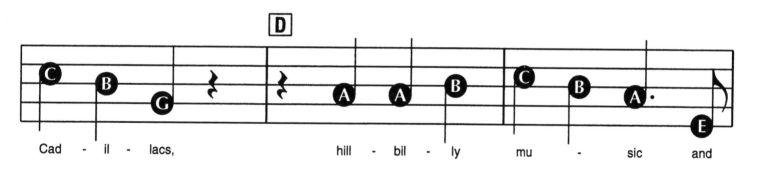

Cad - il - lacs,
hill - bil - ly mu - sic and

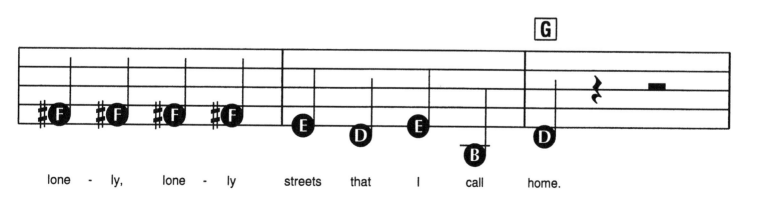

lone - ly, lone - ly streets that I call home.

41

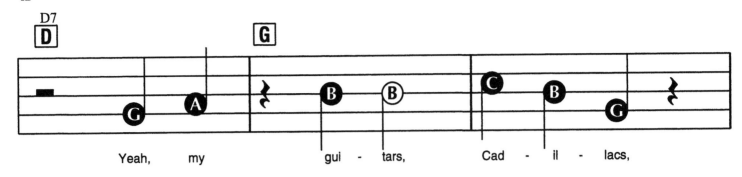

Yeah, my gui - tars, Cad - il - lacs,

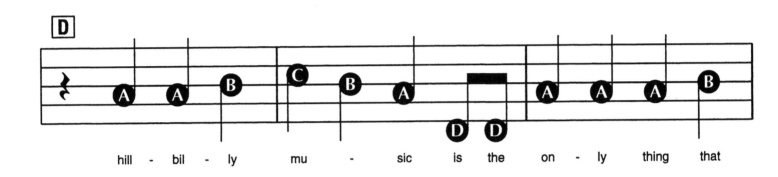

hill - bil - ly mu - sic is the on - ly thing that

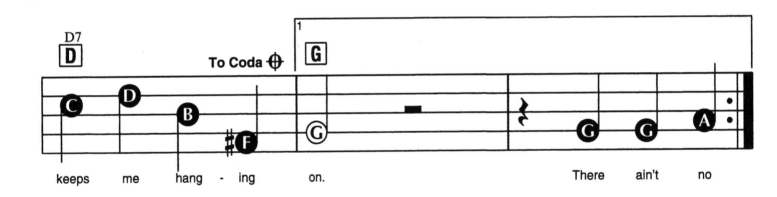

To Coda

keeps me hang - ing on. There ain't no

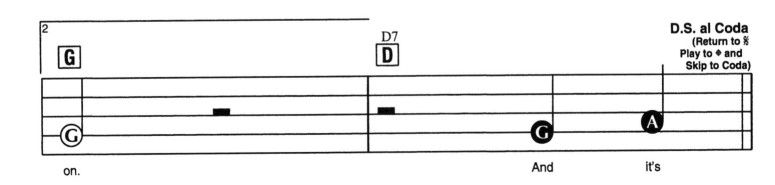

D.S. al Coda
(Return to %
Play to ⊕ and
Skip to Coda)

on. And it's

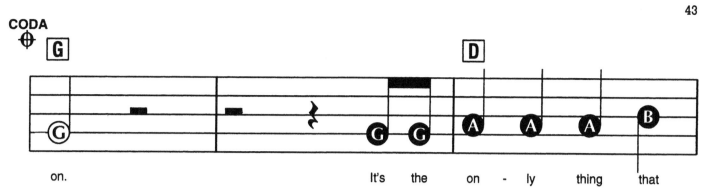

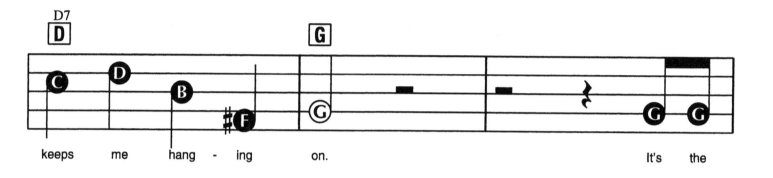

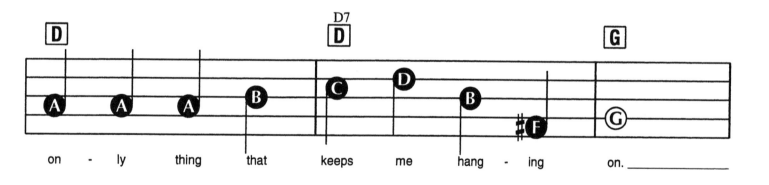

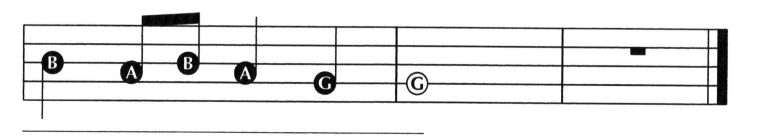

Hey, Good Lookin'

Registration 7
Rhythm: Country Swing or Fox Trot

Words and Music by
Hank Williams

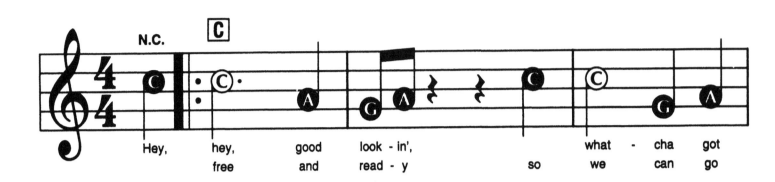

Hey, hey, good look - in', what - cha got
free and read - y so we can go

cook - in', how's a - bout cook - in' some - thin' up with me. ____
stead - y, how's a - bout sav - in' all your time for me. ____

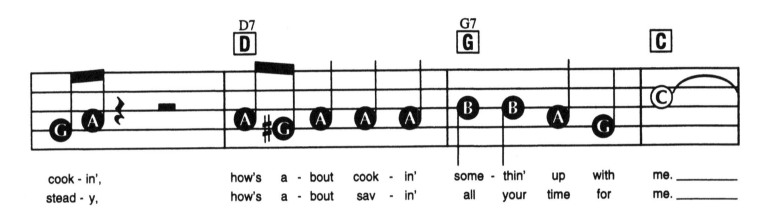

____ Hey, sweet ba - by, don't you think may - be,
____ No more look - in', I know I've been took - en,

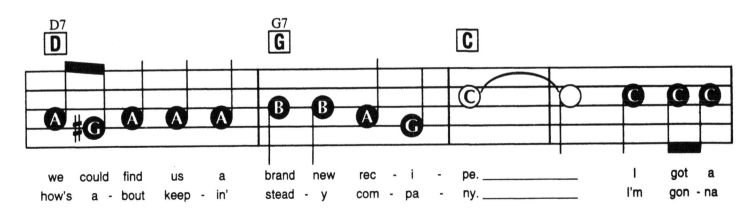

we could find us a brand new rec - i - pe. ____ I got a
how's a - bout keep - in' stead - y com - pa - ny. ____ I'm gon - na

I Think I'll Just Stay Here and Drink

Registration 9
Rhythm: Ballad

Words and Music by
Merle Haggard

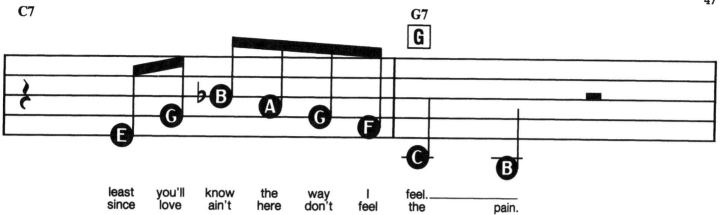

least you'll know the way I feel._____
since love ain't here don't I feel the pain.

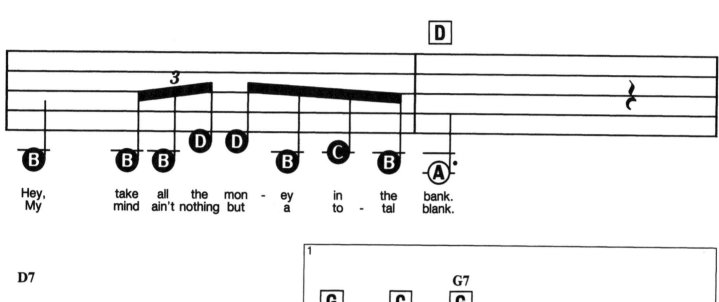

Hey, take all the mon - ey in the bank.
My mind ain't nothing but a to - tal blank.

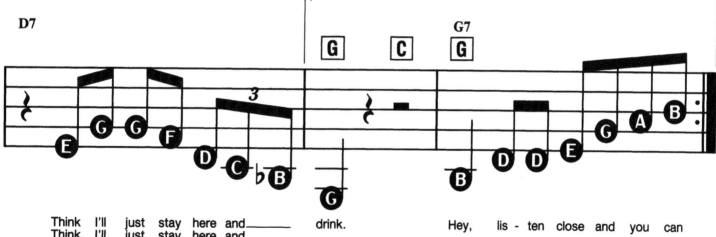

Think I'll just stay here and_____ drink.
Think I'll just stay here and_____

Hey, lis - ten close and you can

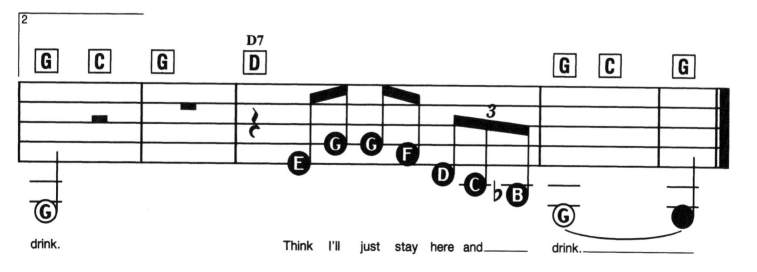

drink.

Think I'll just stay here and_____ drink._____

Jolene

Registration 7
Rhythm: Country Pop or 8-Beat

Words and Music by
Dolly Parton

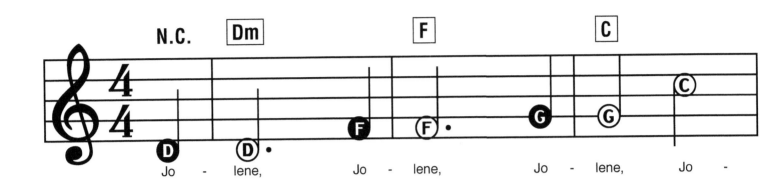

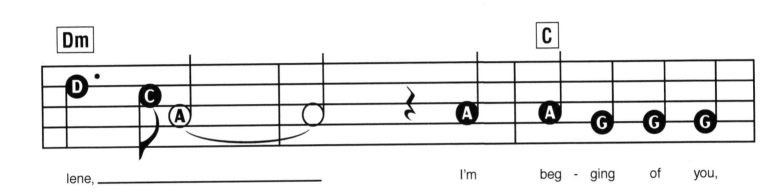

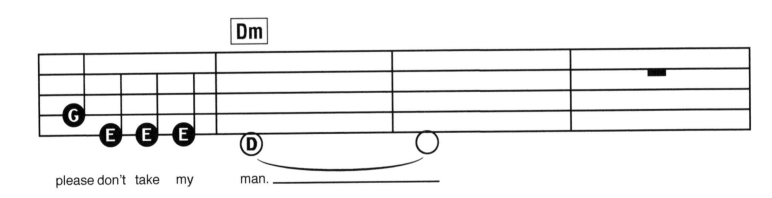

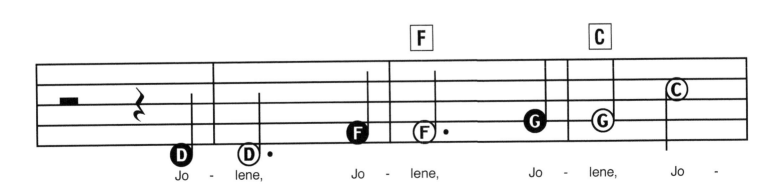

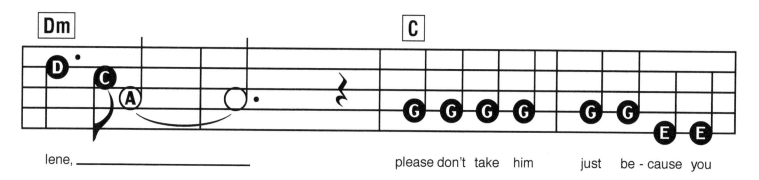

lene, _____ please don't take him just be - cause you

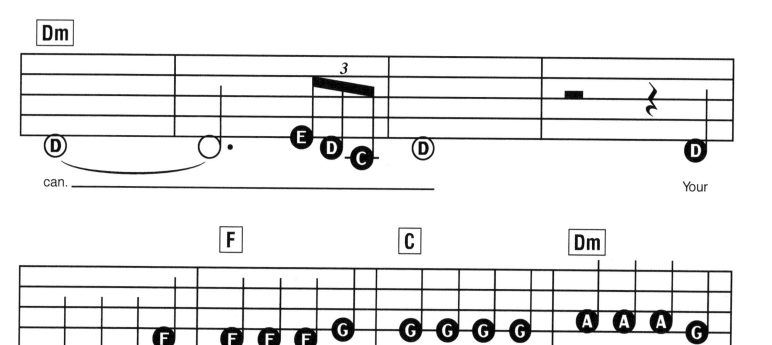

can. _____ Your

beau - ty is be - yond com - pare, with flam - ing locks of au - burn hair, with

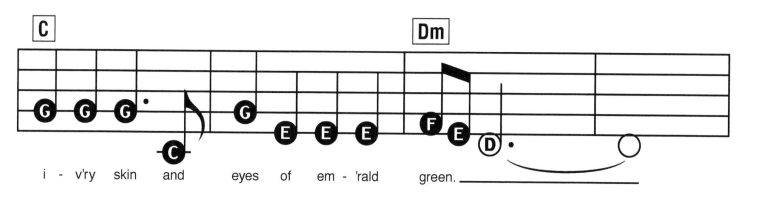

i - v'ry skin and eyes of em - 'rald green. _____

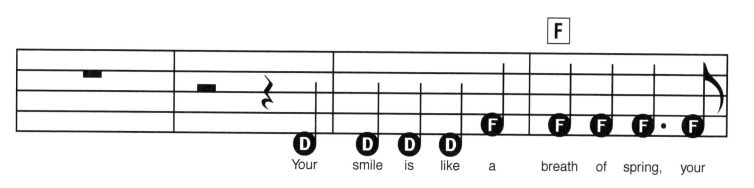

Your smile is like a breath of spring, your

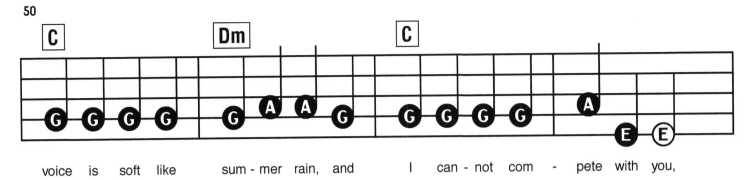

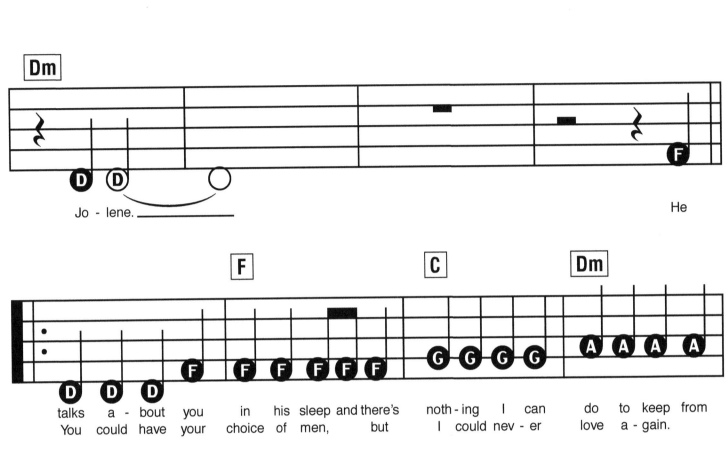

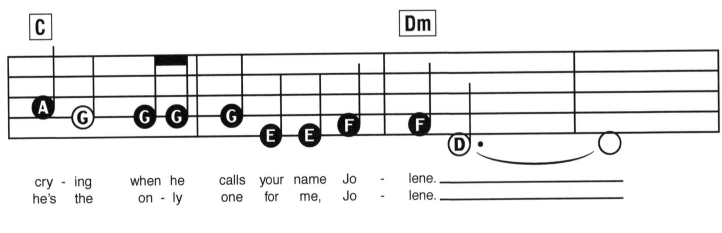

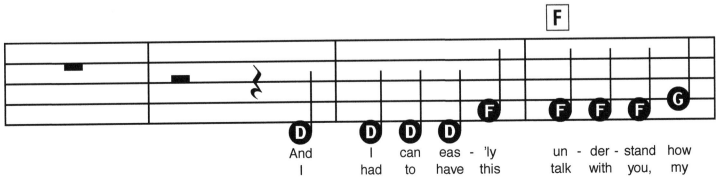

51

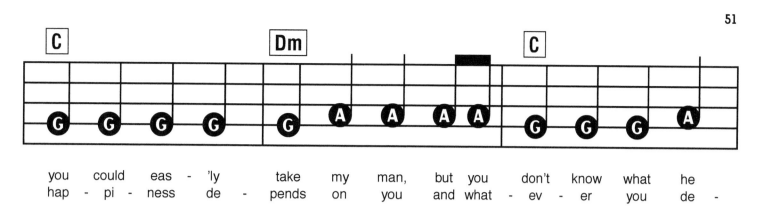

you could eas - 'ly take my man, but you don't know what he
hap - pi - ness de - pends on you and what - ev - er you de -

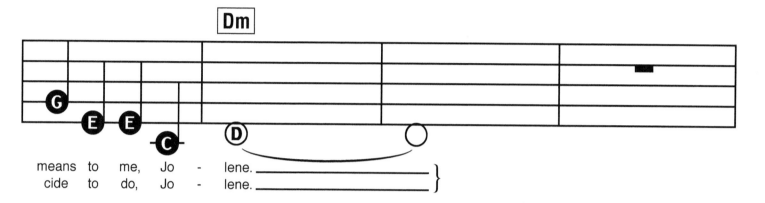

means to me, Jo - lene. _____
cide to do, Jo - lene. _____ }

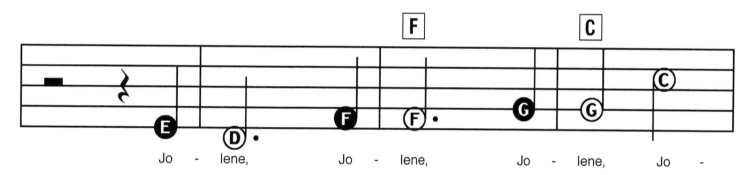

Jo - lene, Jo - lene, Jo - lene, Jo -

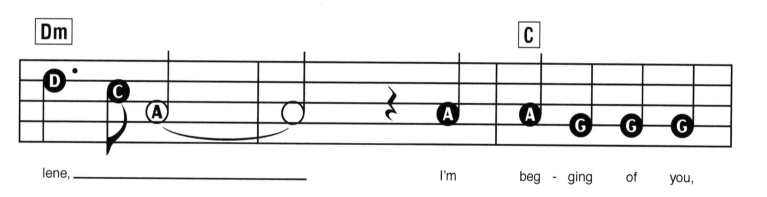

lene, _____ I'm beg - ging of you,

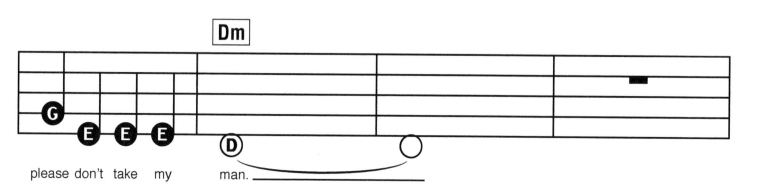

please don't take my man. _____

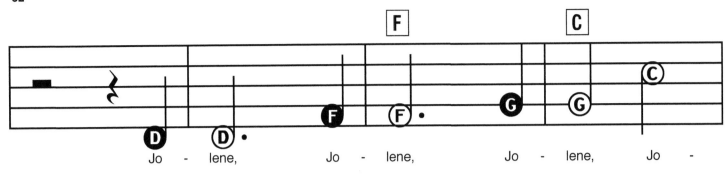

Jo - lene, Jo - lene, Jo - lene, Jo -

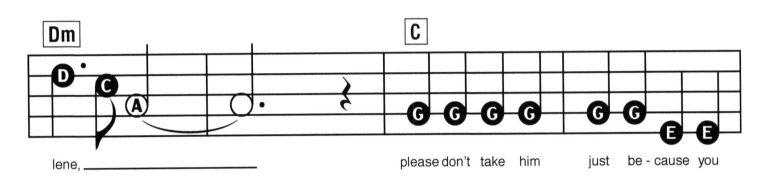

lene, _____ please don't take him just be - cause you

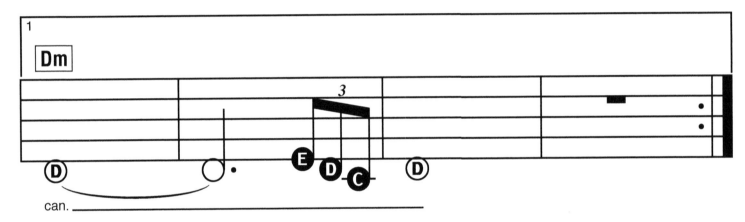

can. _____

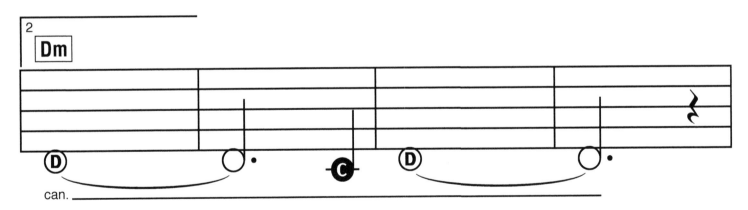

can. _____

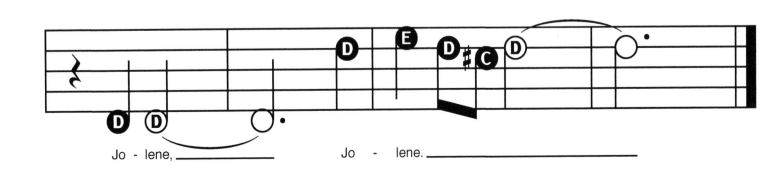

Jo - lene, _____ Jo - lene. _____

My Heroes Have Always Been Cowboys

Registration 9
Rhythm: Waltz

Words and Music by
Sharon Vaughn

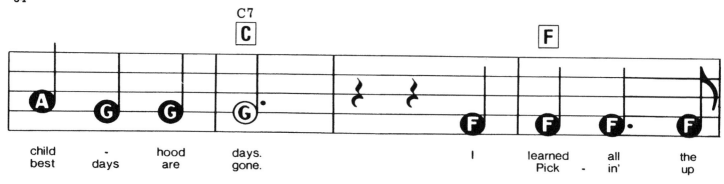

child - hood days.
best days are gone.

I
learned all the
Pick - in' up

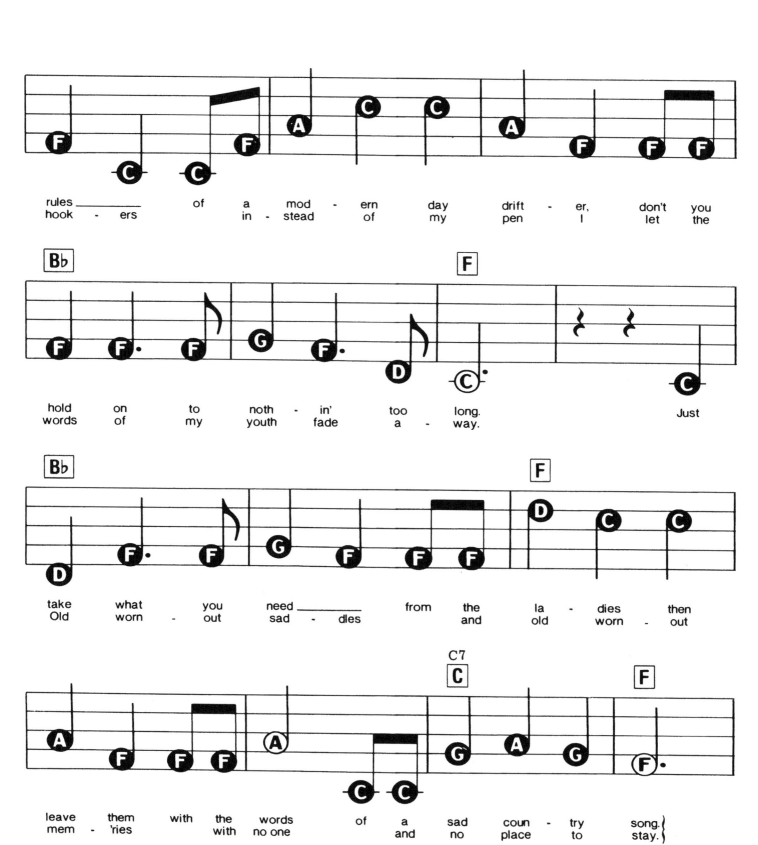

rules _____ of a mod - ern day drift - er, don't you
hook - ers in - stead of my pen I let you the

hold on to noth - in' too long.
words of my youth fade a - way.

Just

take what you need _____ from the la - dies then
Old worn - out sad - dles and old worn - out

leave them with the words of a sad coun - try song.
mem - 'ries with no one and no place to stay.

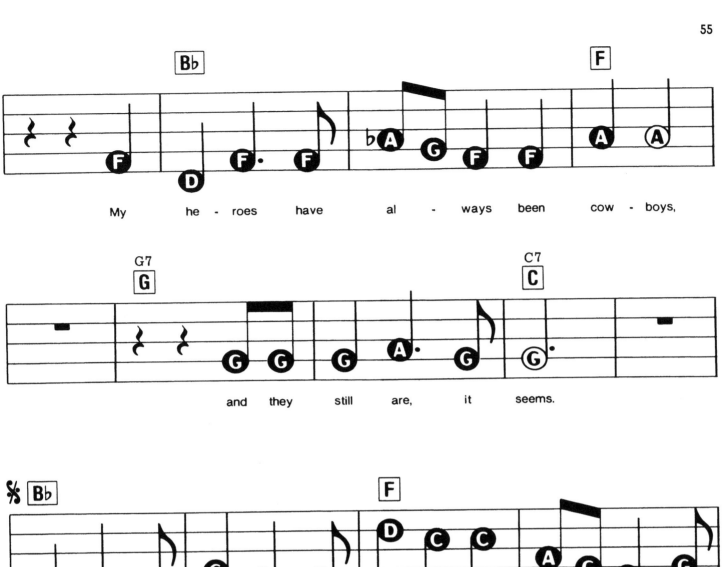

My he - roes have al - ways been cow - boys,

and they still are, it seems.

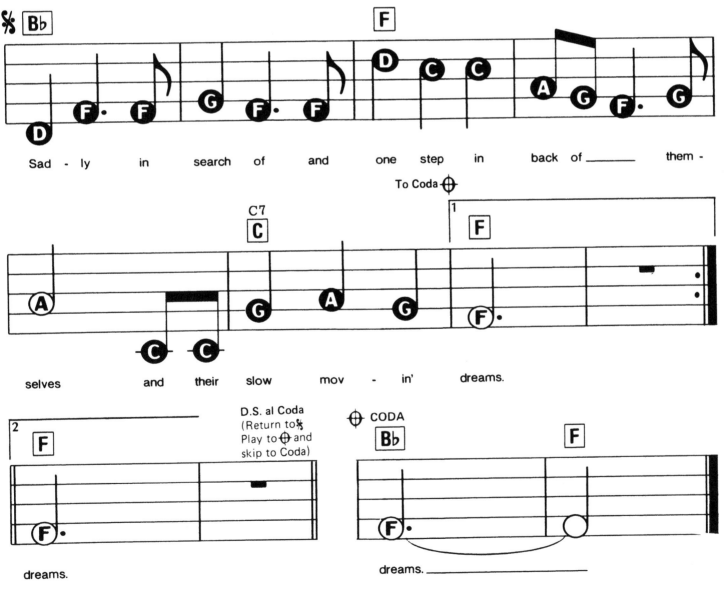

Sad - ly in search of and one step in back of _____ them -

To Coda

selves and their slow mov - in' dreams.

D.S. al Coda
(Return to 𝄋
Play to ✛ and
skip to Coda)

✛ CODA

dreams.

dreams. _____

King of the Road

Registration 7
Rhythm: Country

Words and Music by
Roger Miller

57

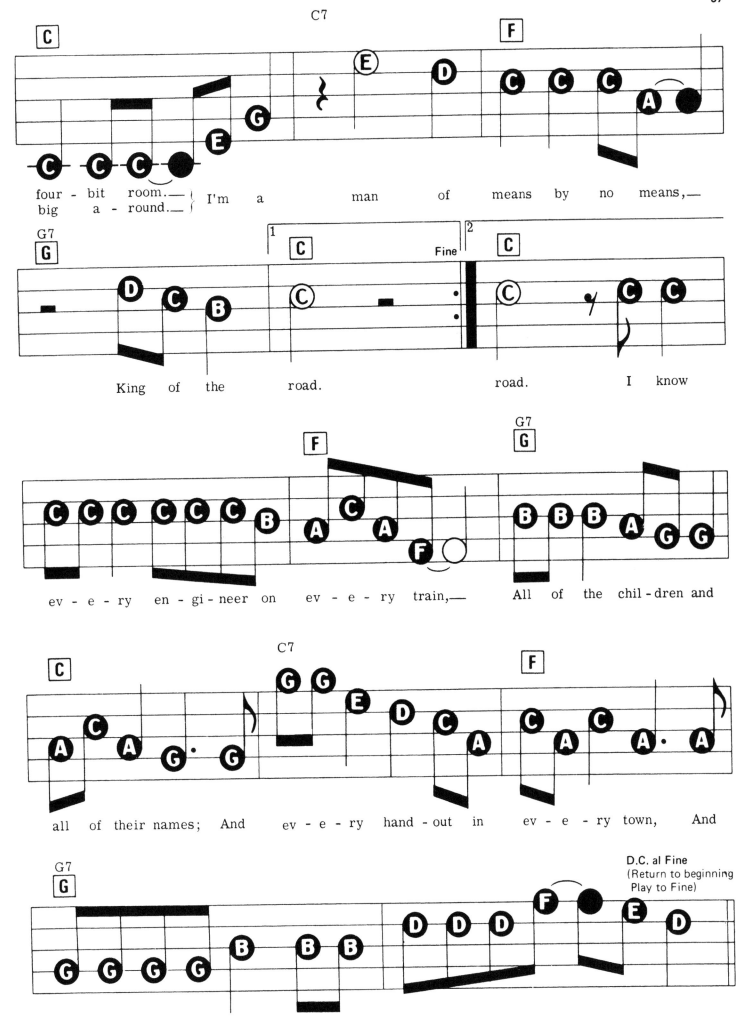

Long Haired Country Boy

Registration 4
Rhythm: Country Shuffle or Country

Words and Music by
Charlie Daniels

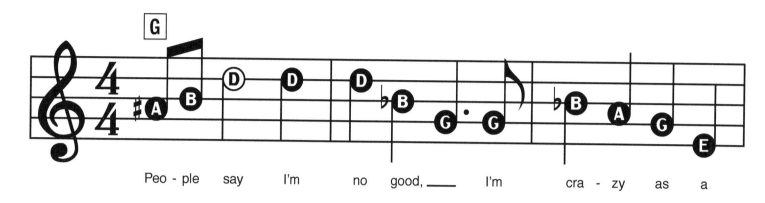

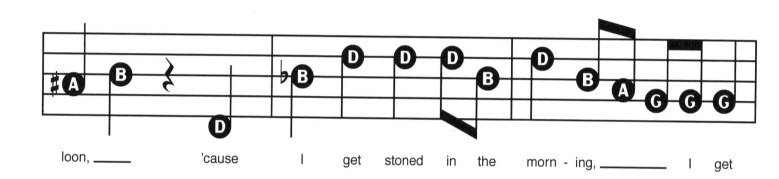

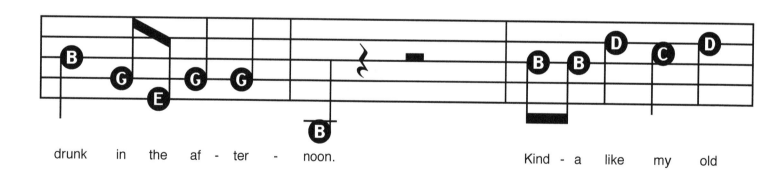

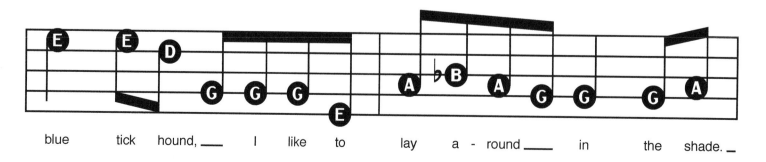

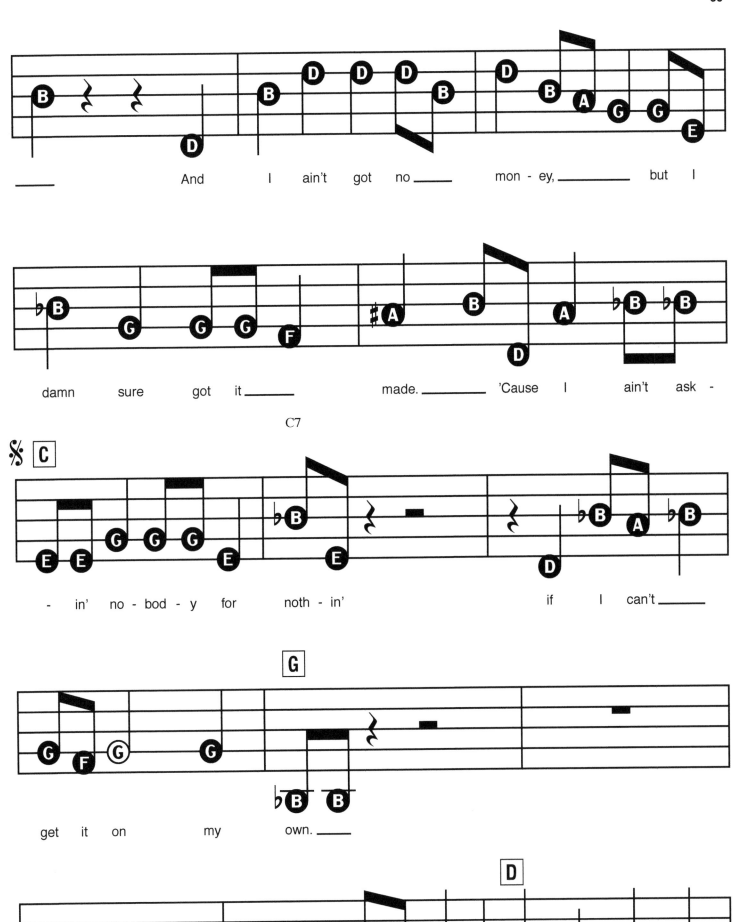

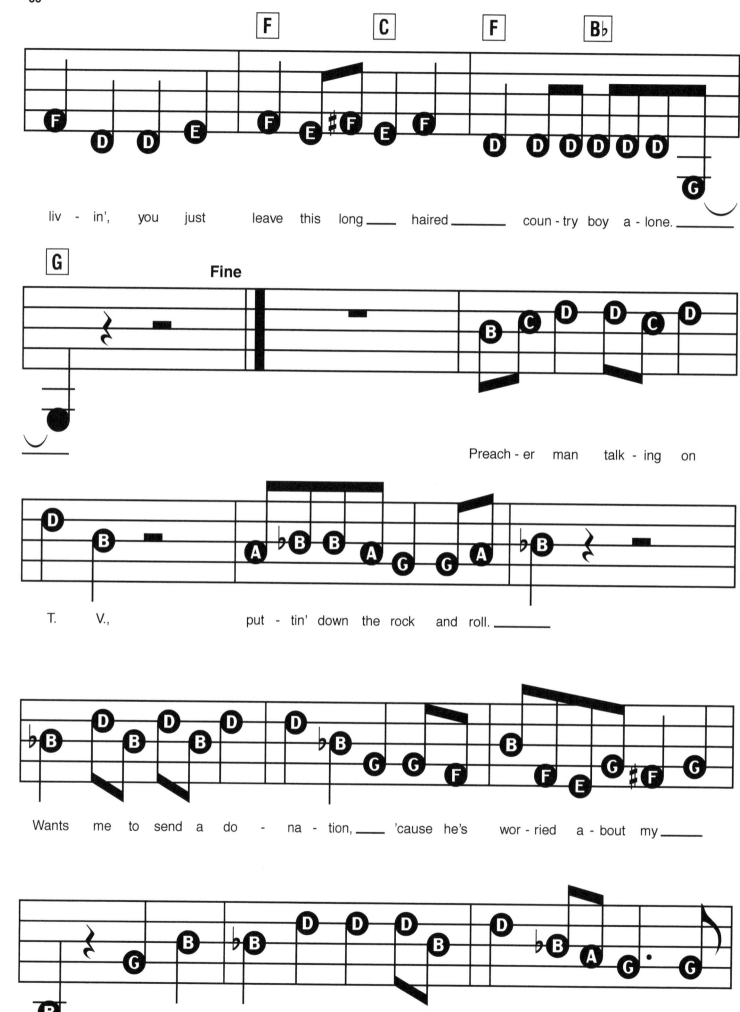

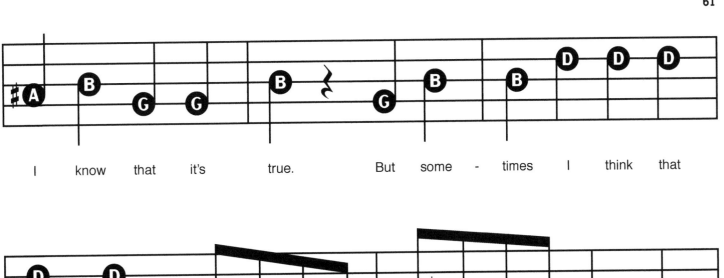

I know that it's true. But some - times I think that

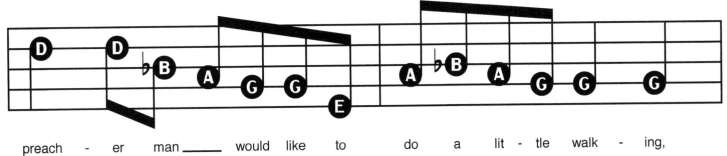

preach - er man _____ would like to do a lit - tle walk - ing,

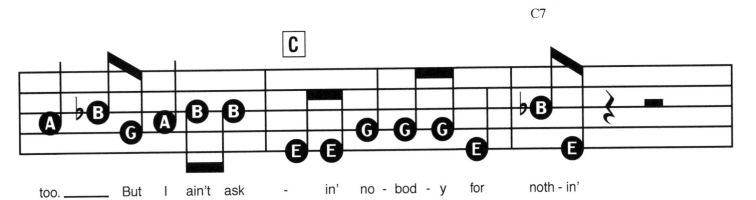

too. _____ But I ain't ask - in' no - bod - y for noth - in'

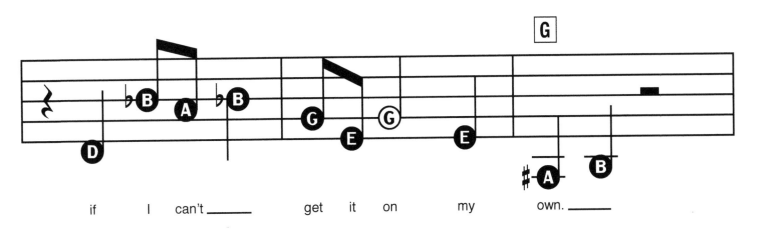

if I can't _____ get it on my own. _____

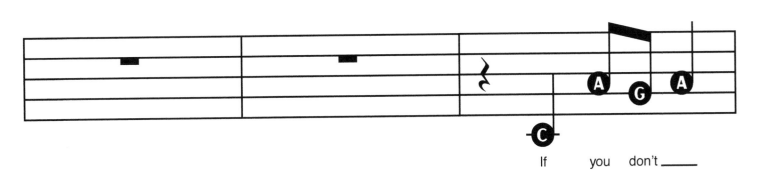

If you don't _____

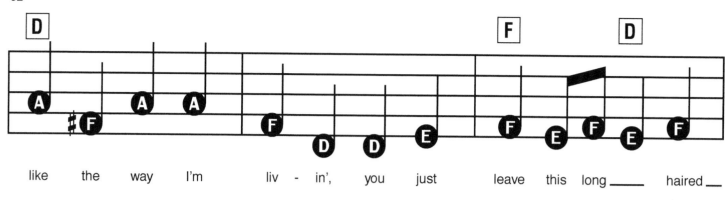

like the way I'm liv - in', you just leave this long ____ haired ____

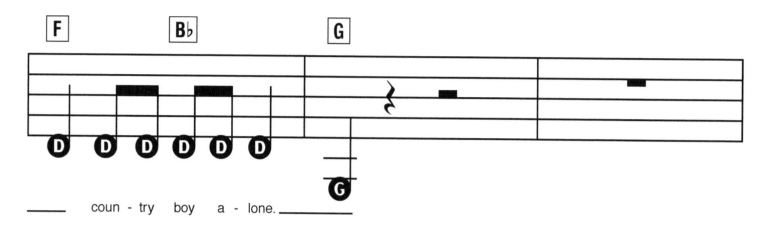

____ coun - try boy a - lone. ____

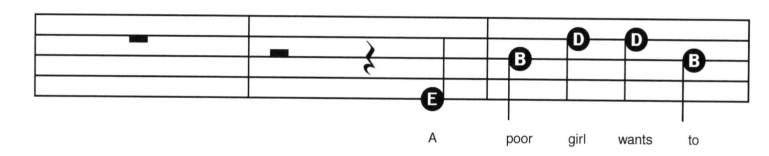

A poor girl wants to

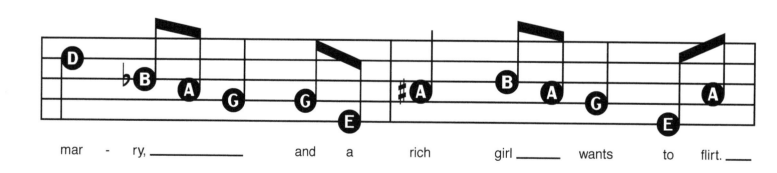

mar - ry, ____ and a rich girl ____ wants to flirt. ____

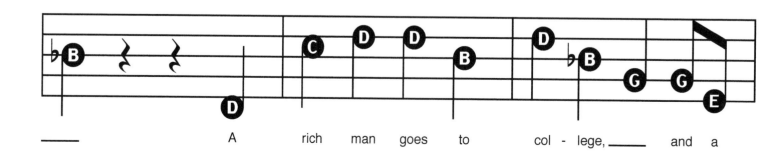

____ A rich man goes to col - lege, ____ and a

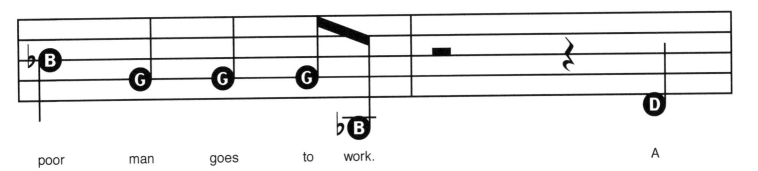

poor   man   goes   to   work.   A

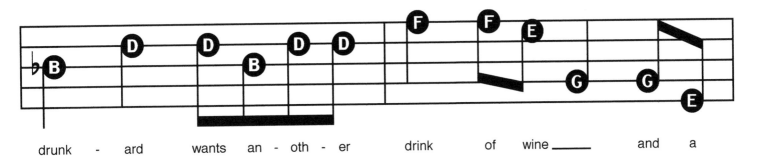

drunk - ard   wants   an - oth - er   drink   of   wine _____   and   a

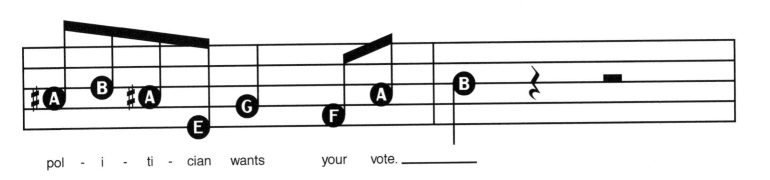

pol - i - ti - cian   wants   your   vote. _____

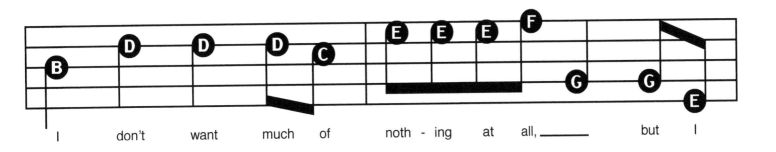

I   don't   want   much   of   noth - ing   at   all, _____   but   I

D.S. al Fine
(Return to 𝄋
Play to Fine)

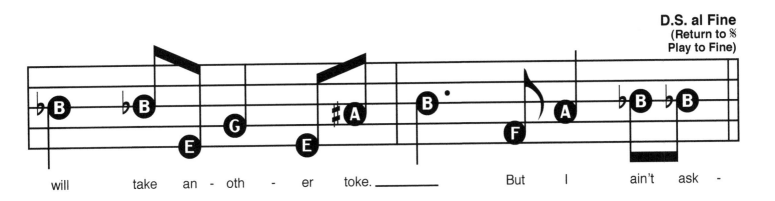

will   take   an - oth - er   toke. _____   But   I   ain't   ask -

Louisiana Woman, Mississippi Man

Registration 8
Rhythm: Country Rock or 8-Beat

Words and Music by Jim Owen
and Becki Bluefield

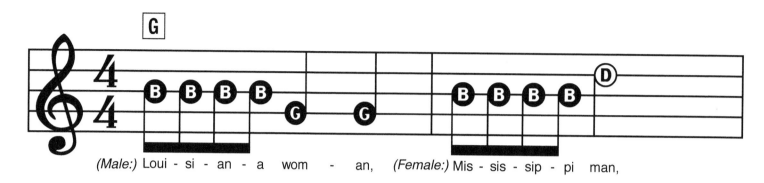

(Male:) Loui - si - an - a wom - an, (Female:) Mis - sis - sip - pi man,

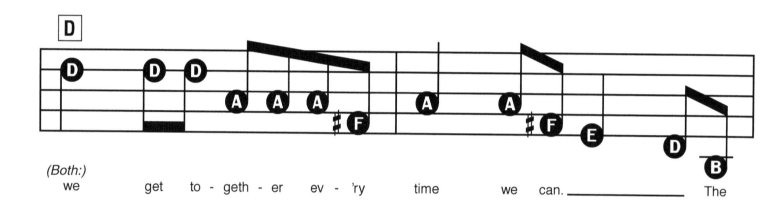

(Both:) we get to - geth - er ev - 'ry time we can. _____ The

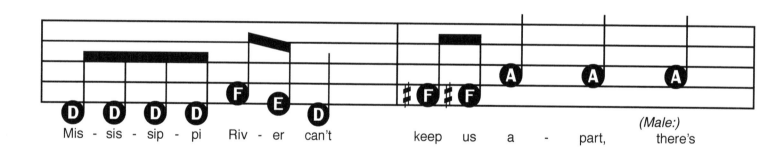

Mis - sis - sip - pi Riv - er can't keep us a - part, (Male:) there's

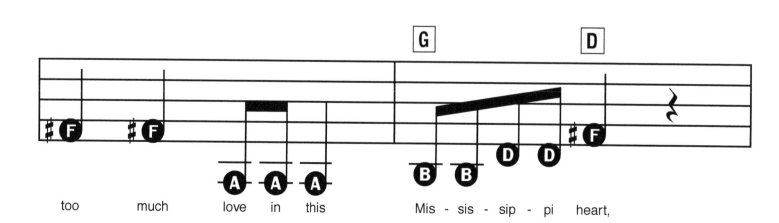

too much love in this Mis - sis - sip - pi heart,

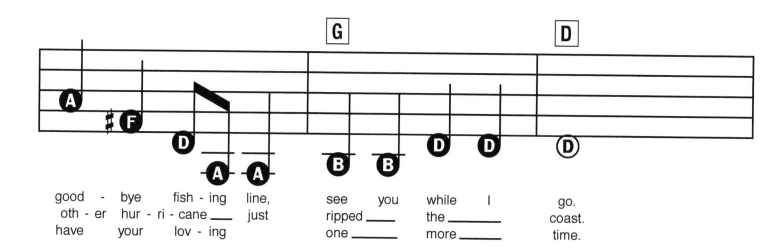

good - bye fish - ing line, see you while I go.
oth - er hur - ri - cane ___ just ripped ___ the ___ coast.
have your lov - ing one ___ more ___ time.

With that Loui - si - an - a wom - an wait - ing
If he can't ___ come to me, ___ I'm a -
(Male:) I'm gon - na jump ___ in the riv - er and a -

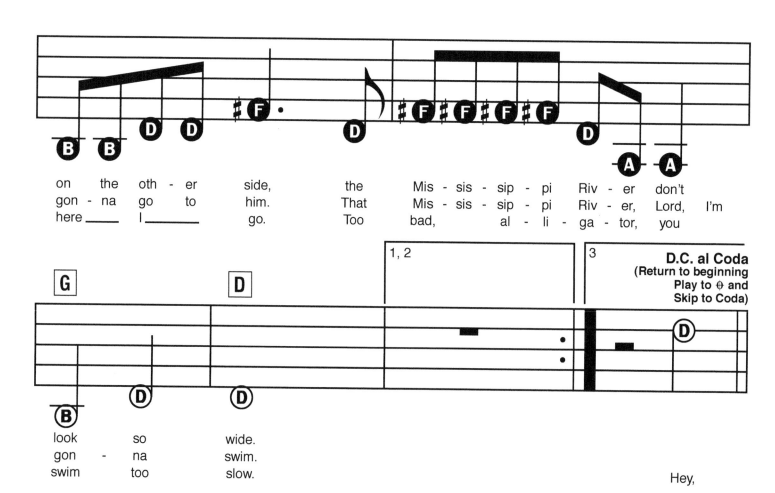

on the oth - er side, the Mis - sis - sip - pi Riv - er don't
gon - na go to him. That Mis - sis - sip - pi Riv - er, Lord, I'm
here ___ I ___ go. Too bad, al - li - ga - tor, you

1, 2

3 **D.C. al Coda**
(Return to beginning
Play to ⊕ and
Skip to Coda)

look so wide.
gon - na swim.
swim too slow.

Hey,

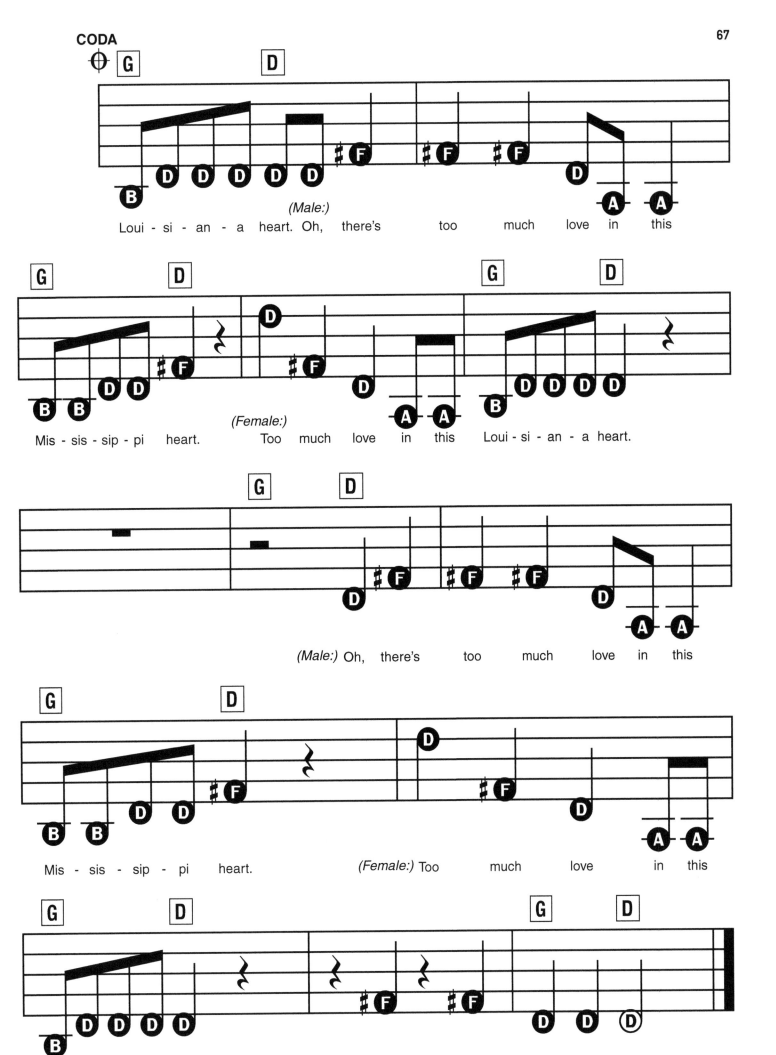

Make the World Go Away

Registration 10
Rhythm: Country

Words and Music by
Hank Cochran

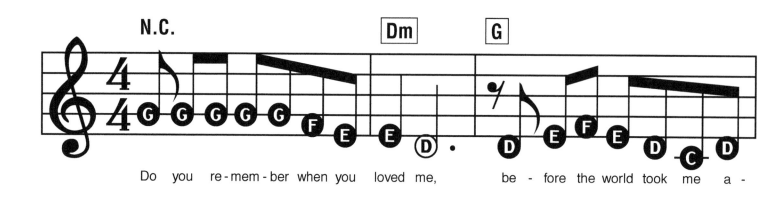

Do you re-mem-ber when you loved me, be - fore the world took me a -

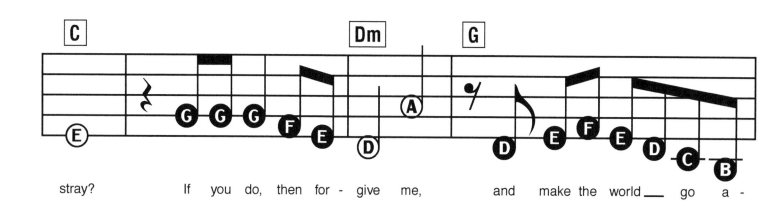

stray? If you do, then for - give me, and make the world ___ go a -

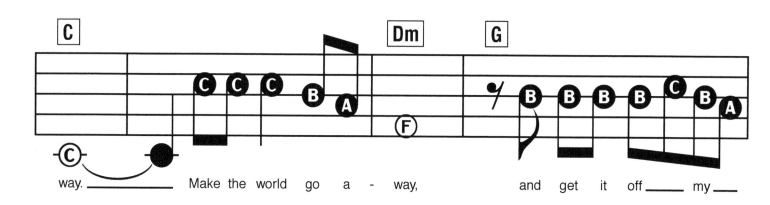

way. _____ Make the world go a - way, and get it off ___ my ___

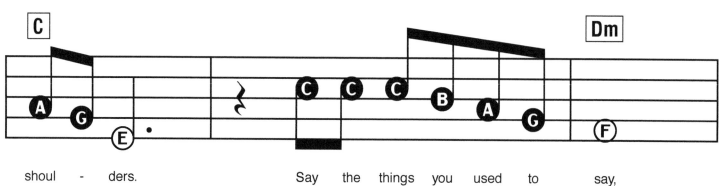

shoul - ders. Say the things you used to say,

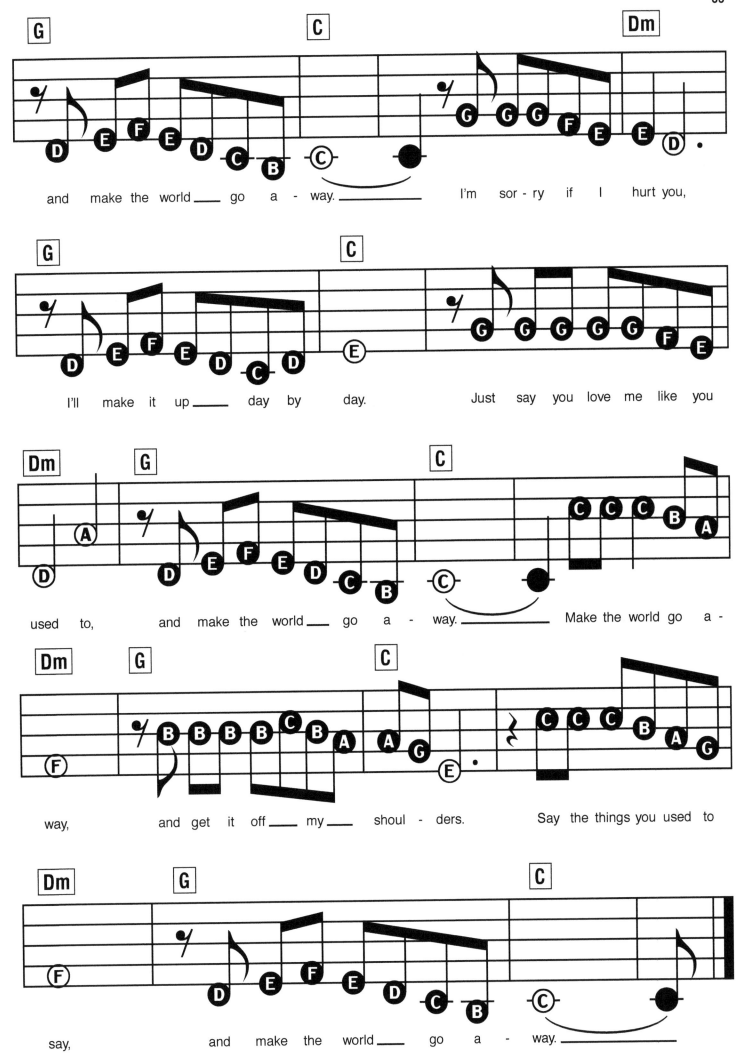

Mama Tried

Registration 7
Rhythm: Rock or Country

Words and Music by
Merle Haggard

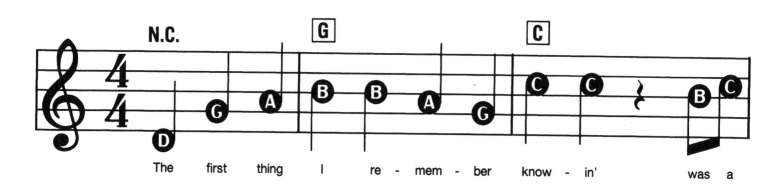

The first thing I re - mem - ber know - in' was a

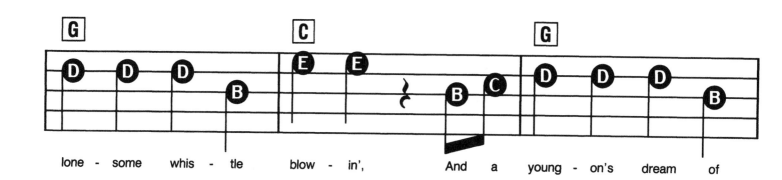

lone - some whis - tle blow - in', And a young - on's dream of

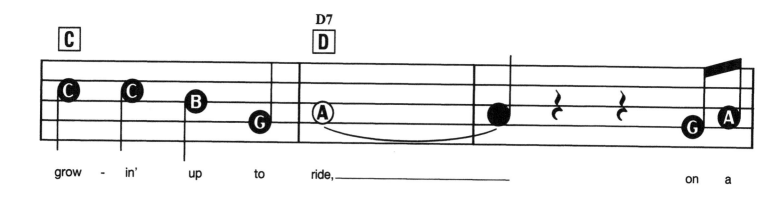

grow - in' up to ride, on a

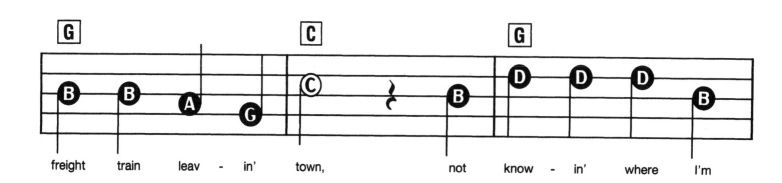

freight train leav - in' town, not know - in' where I'm

71

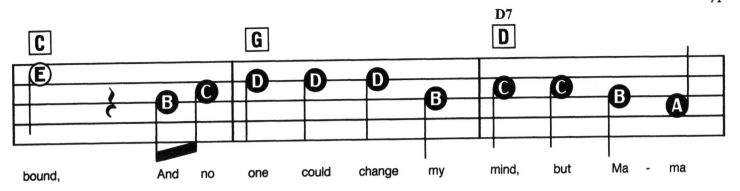

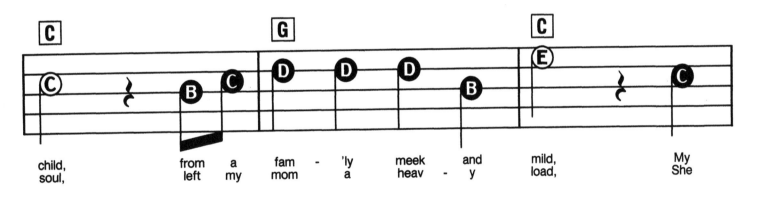

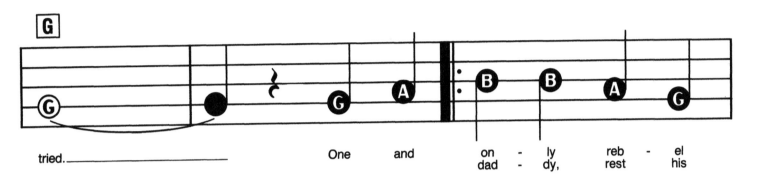

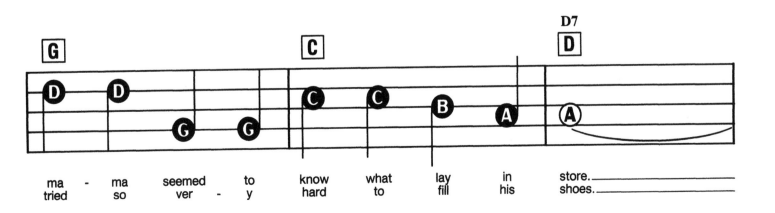

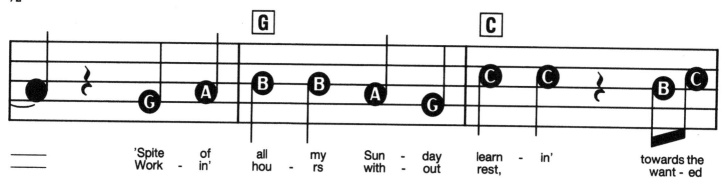

'Spite of all my Sun - day learn - in'
Work - in' hou - rs with - out rest, towards the
want - ed

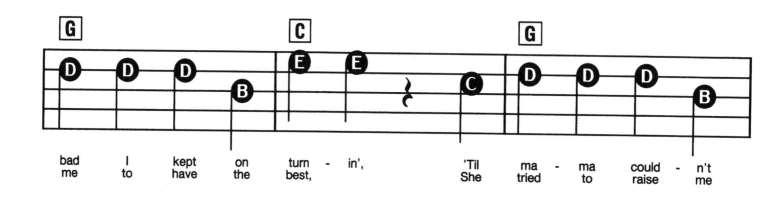

bad I kept on turn - in', 'Til ma - ma could - n't
me to have the best, She tried to raise me

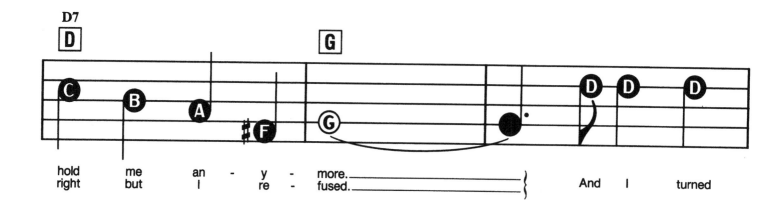

hold me an - y - more. And I turned
right but I re - fused.

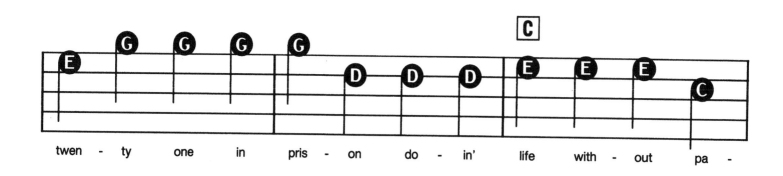

twen - ty one in pris - on do - in' life with - out pa -

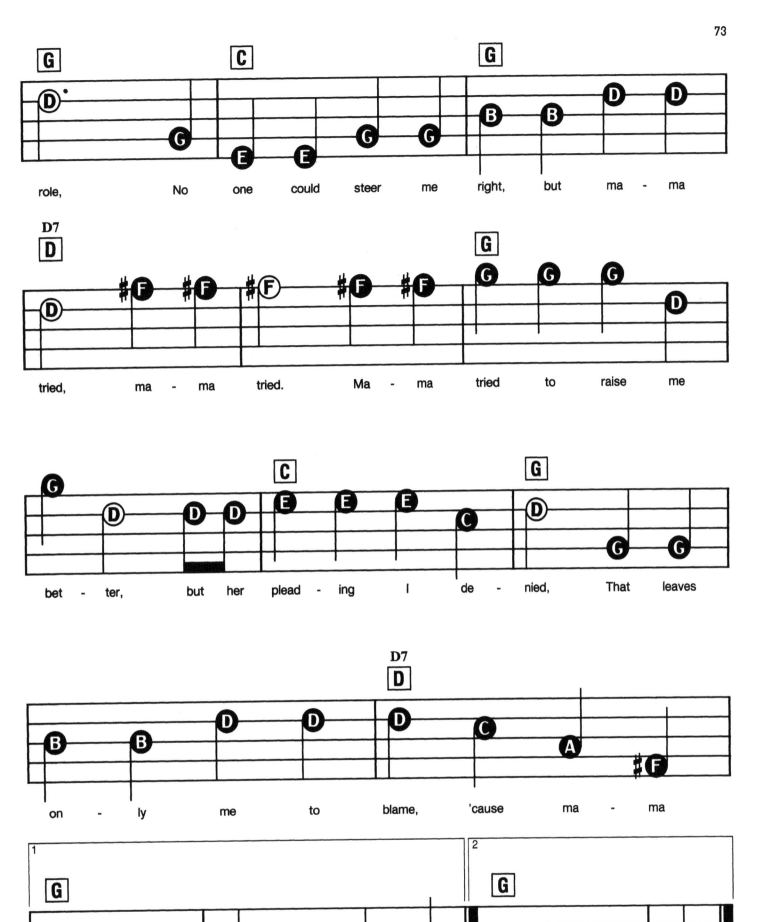

Me and Paul

Registration 4
Rhythm: Country Swing

Words and Music by
Willie Nelson

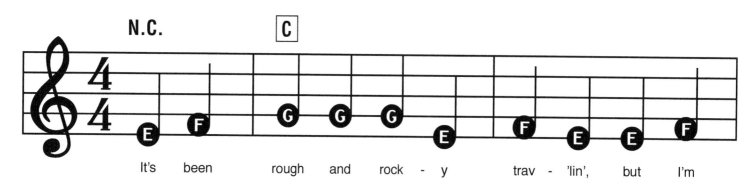

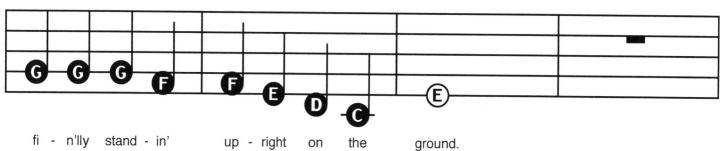

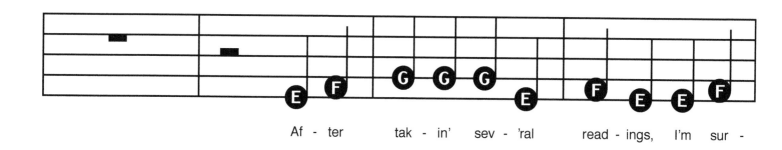

C7

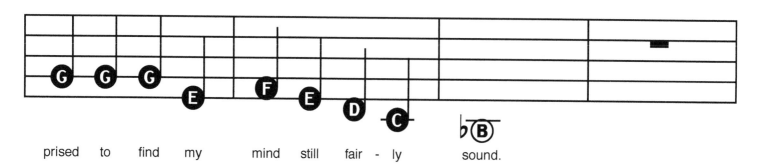

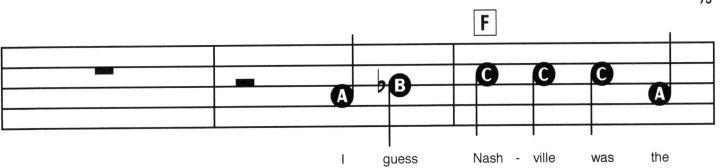

I guess Nash - ville was the

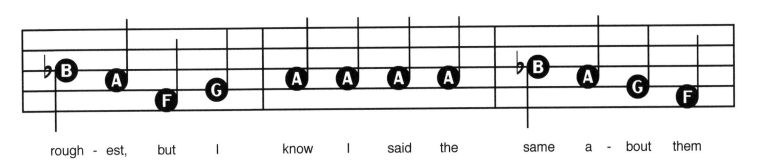

rough - est, but I know I said the same a - bout them

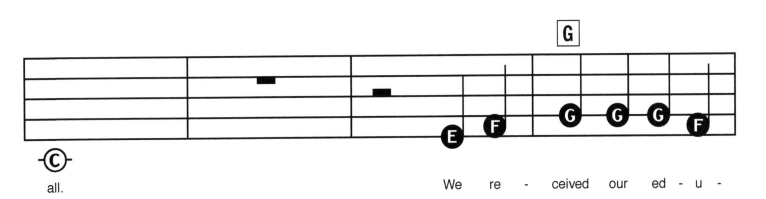

all. We re - ceived our ed - u -

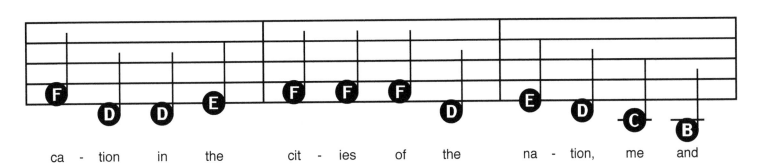

ca - tion in the cit - ies of the na - tion, me and

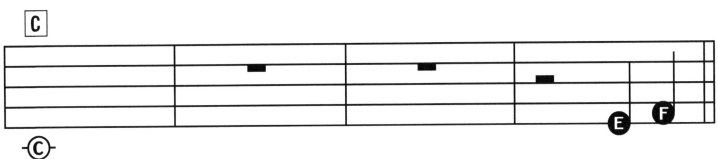

Paul. Al - most

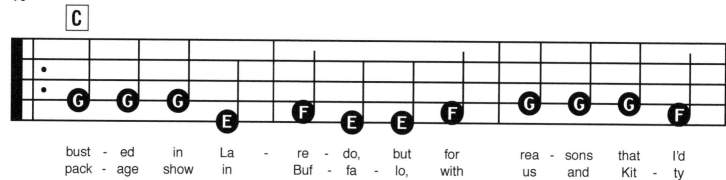

C											
G	G	G	E	F	E	E	F	G	G	G	F

bust - ed in La - re - do, but for rea - sons that I'd
pack - age show in Buf - fa - lo, with us and Kit - ty

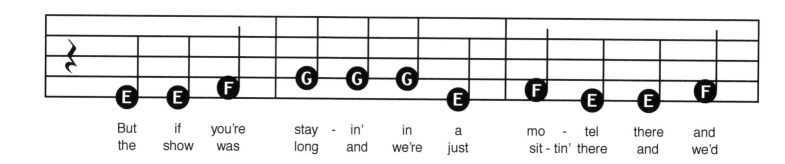

F E D C E

rath - er not dis - close.
Wells and Char - lie Pride,

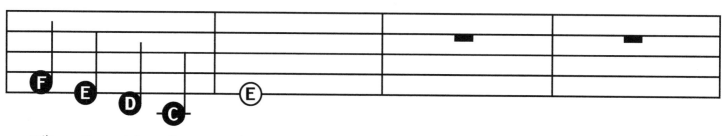

E E F G G G E F E E F

But if you're stay - in' in a mo - tel there and
the show was long and we're just sit - tin' there and we'd

C7

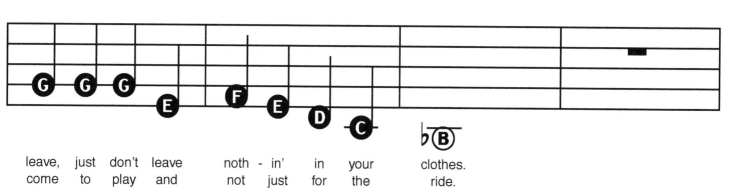

G G G E F E D C ♭B

leave, just don't leave noth - in' in your clothes.
come to play and not just for the ride.

F

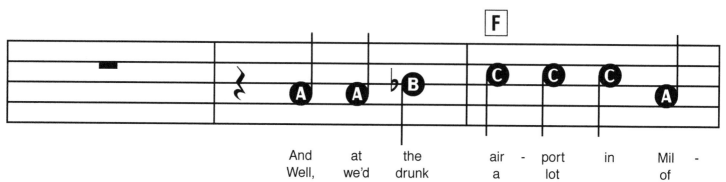

A A ♭B C C C A

And at the air - port in Mil -
Well, we'd drunk a lot of

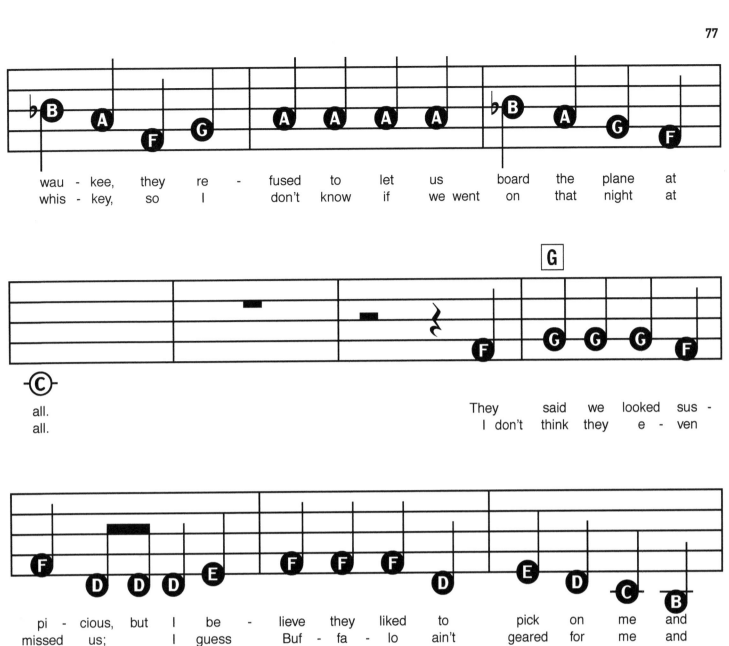

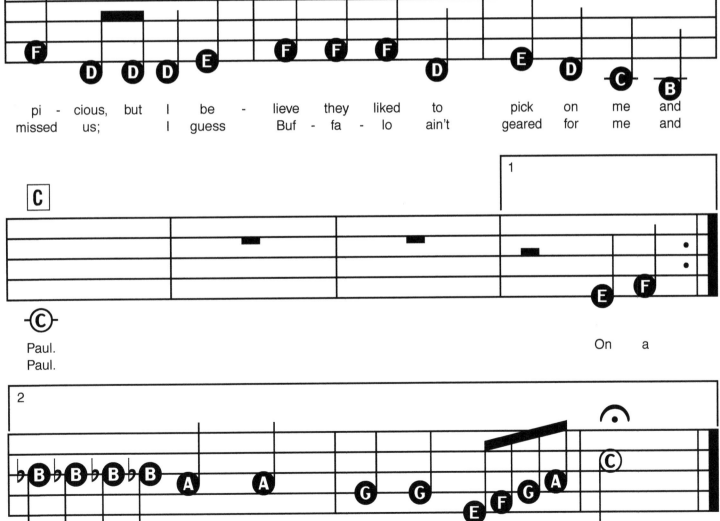

(Instrumental)

Nine to Five
from NINE TO FIVE

Registration 5
Rhythm: Rock

Words and Music by
Dolly Parton

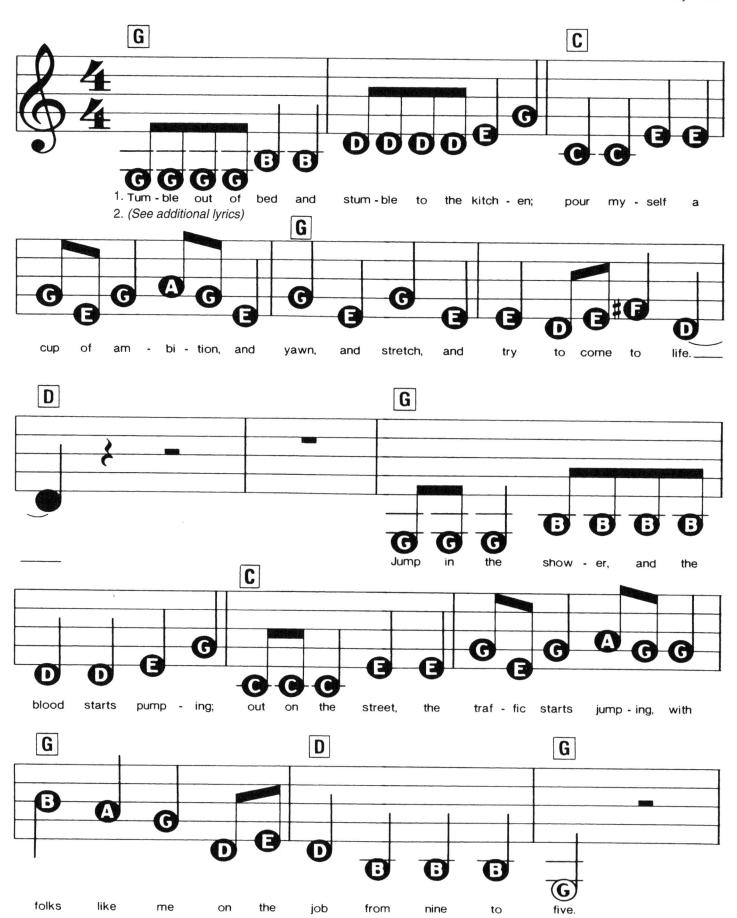

Chorus

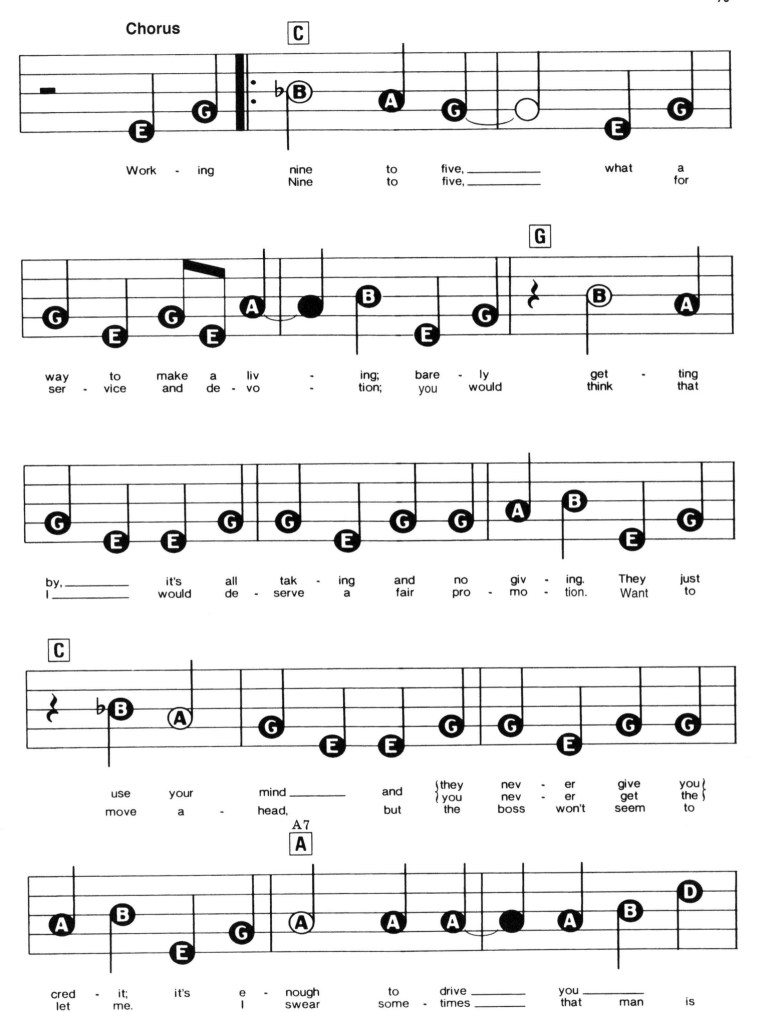

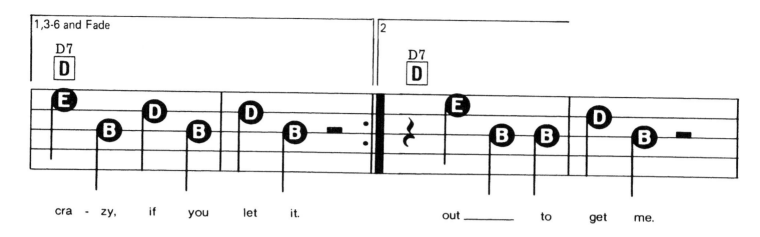

cra - zy,   if   you   let   it.   out _____ to   get   me.

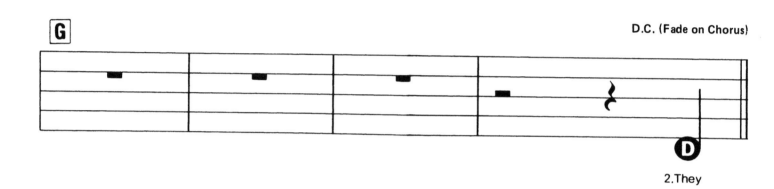

D.C. (Fade on Chorus)

2. They

Additional Lyrics

Verse 2:

They let you dream just to watch them shatter;
You're just a step on the boss man's ladder,
But you've got dreams he'll never take away.
In the same boat with a lot of your friends;
Waitin' for the day your ship'll come in,
And the tide's gonna turn, and it's all gonna roll your way.
Chorus

Chorus 4,6:

Nine to five, they've got you where they want you;
There's a better life, and you dream about it, don't you?
It's a rich man's game, no matter what they call it;
And you spend your life putting money in his pocket.

Streets of Bakersfield

Registration 7
Rhythm: Country or Rock

Words and Music by
Homer Joy

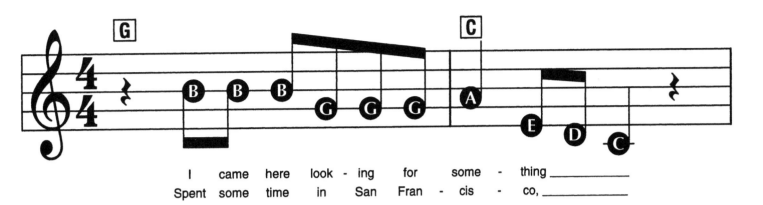

I came here look-ing for some - thing _____
Spent some time in San Fran - cis - co, _____

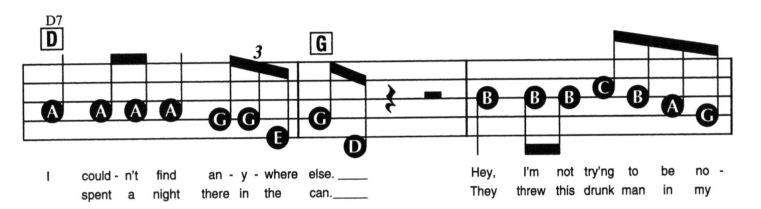

I could - n't find an - y - where else. _____
spent a night there in the can. _____

Hey, I'm not try'ng to be no -
They threw this drunk man in my

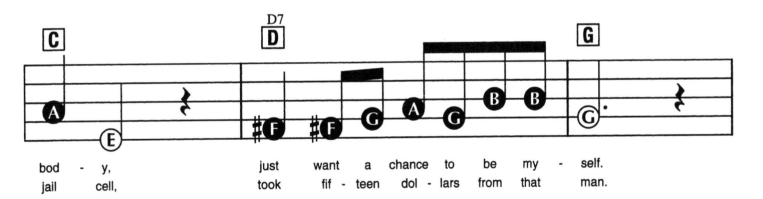

bod - y,
jail cell,

just want a chance to be my - self.
took fif - teen dol - lars from that man.

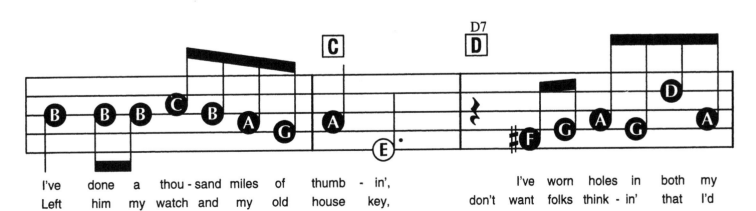

I've done a thou - sand miles of thumb - in',
Left him my watch and my old house key,

I've worn holes in both my
don't want folks think - in' that I'd

82

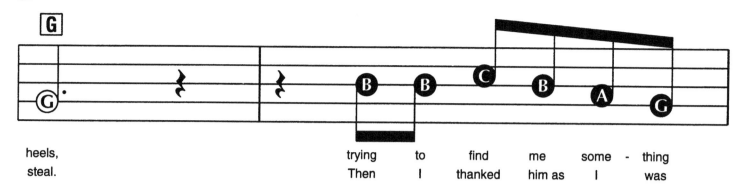

heels,
steal.
trying to find me some - thing
Then I thanked him as I was

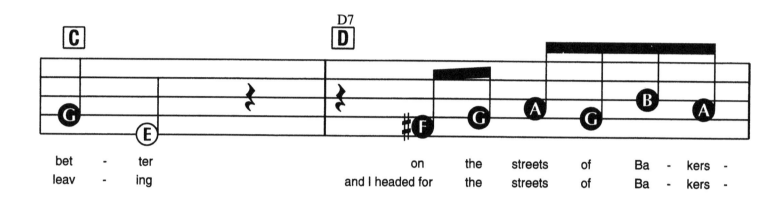

bet - ter
leav - ing
on the streets of Ba - kers -
and I headed for the streets of Ba - kers -

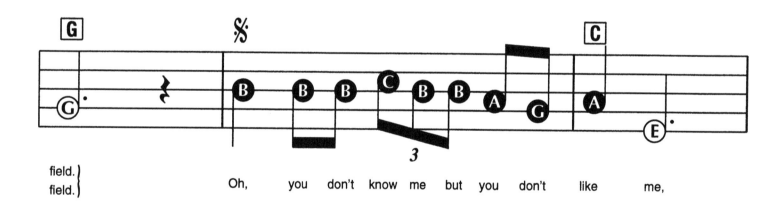

field.)
field.)
Oh, you don't know me but you don't like me,

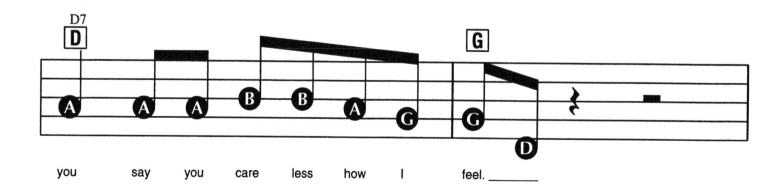

you say you care less how I feel. _____

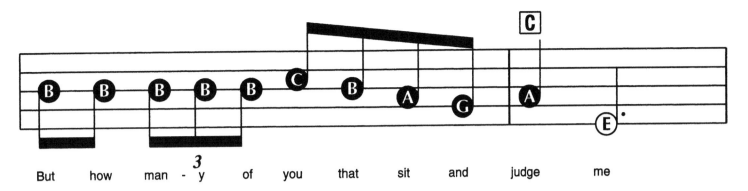

But how man - y of you that sit and judge me

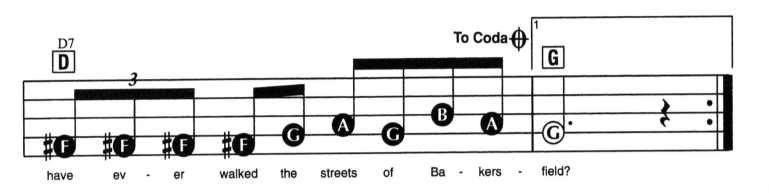

have ev - er walked the streets of Ba - kers - field?

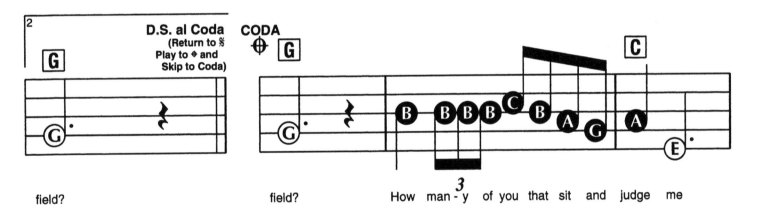

field?

field? How man - y of you that sit and judge me

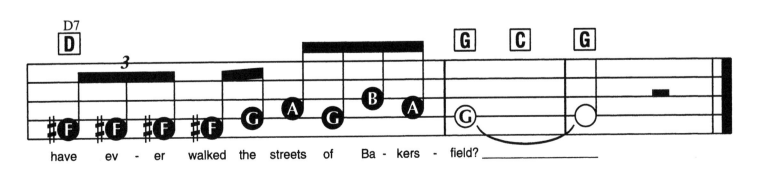

have ev - er walked the streets of Ba - kers - field? _____

On the Road Again

Registration 7
Rhythm: Swing

Words and Music by
Willie Nelson

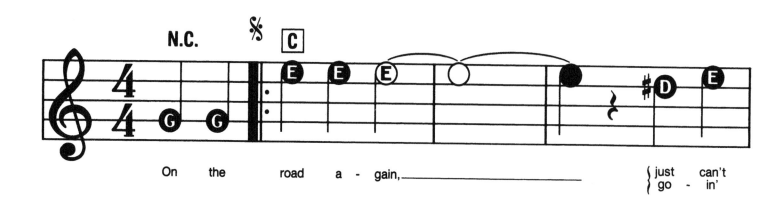

On the road a - gain,_____ { just can't
go - in'

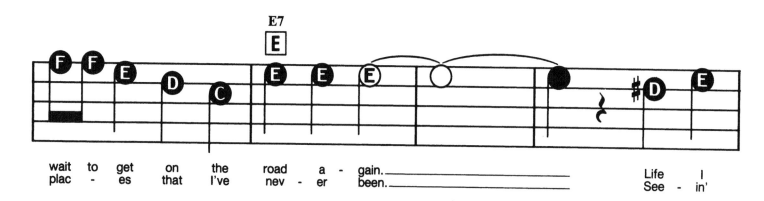

wait to get on the road a - gain._____ Life I
plac - es that I've nev - er been._____ See - in'

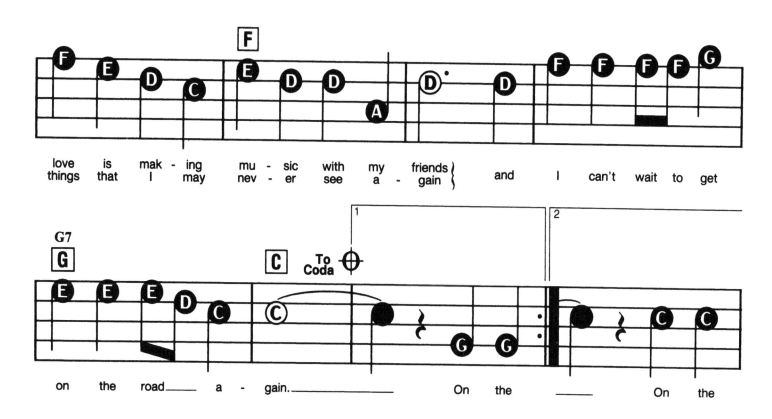

love is mak - ing mu - sic with my friends } and I can't wait to get
things that I may nev - er see a - gain {

on the road_____ a - gain._____ On the _____ On the

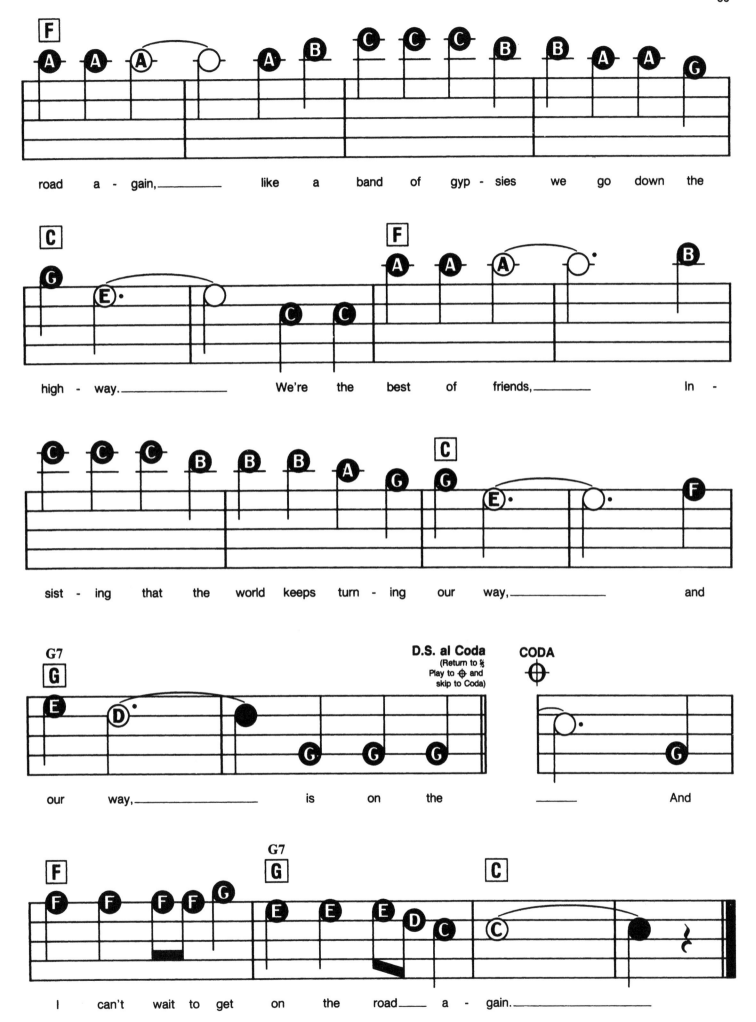

Rednecks, White Socks and Blue Ribbon Beer

Registration 4
Rhythm: Rock or 8-Beat

Words and Music by Chuck Neese,
Bob McDill and Wayland Holyfield

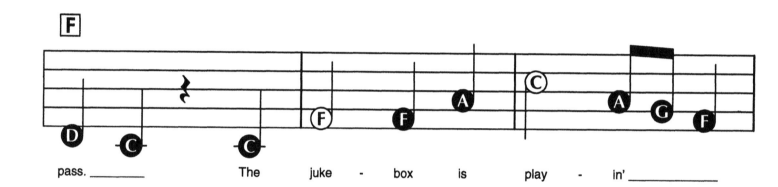

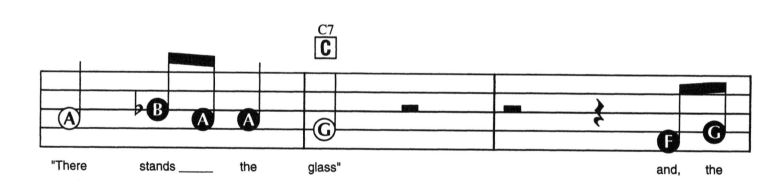

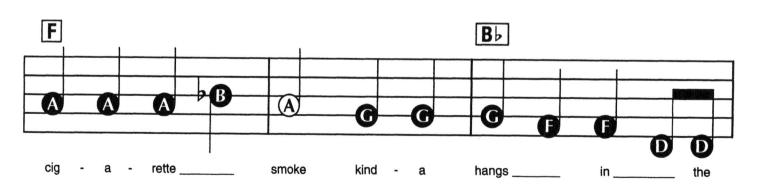

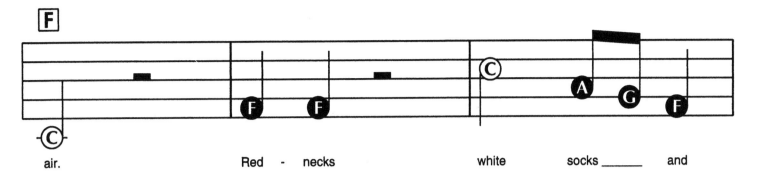

air.　　　Red - necks　　white　socks _____ and

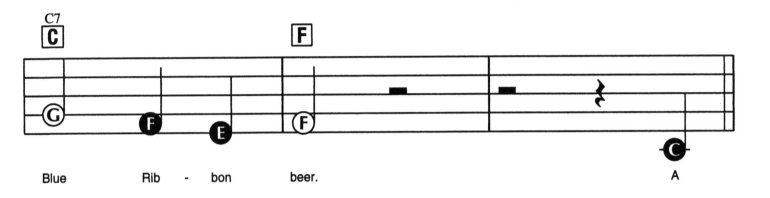

Blue　Rib - bon　beer.　　　　　A

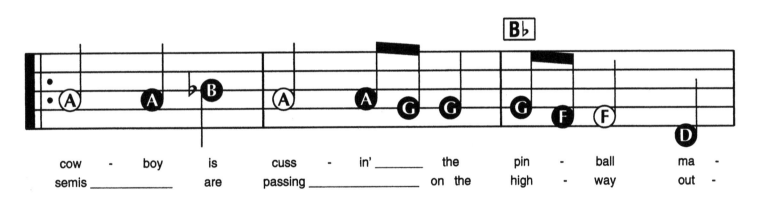

cow - boy　is　cuss - in' _____ the　pin - ball　ma -
semis _____ are　passing _____ on the　high - way　out -

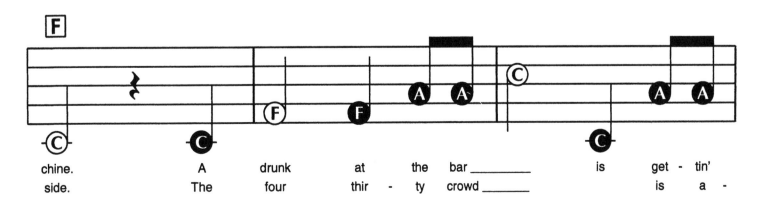

chine.　　A　drunk　at　the　bar _____　is　get - tin'
side.　　The　four　thir - ty　crowd _____　is　a -

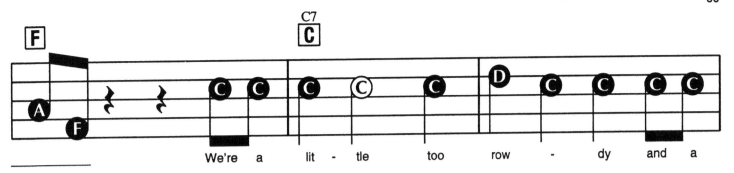

We're a lit - tle too row - dy and a

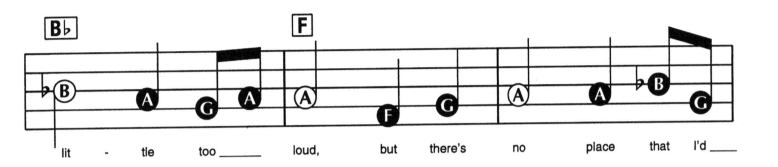

lit - tle too _____ loud, but there's no place that I'd ____

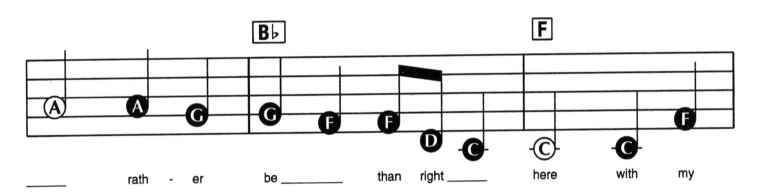

_____ rath - er be _____ than right _____ here with my

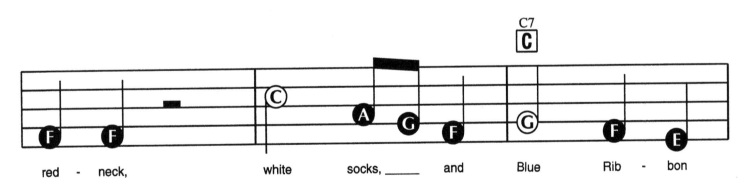

red - neck, white socks, _____ and Blue Rib - bon

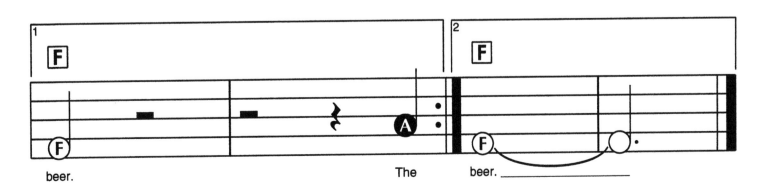

beer. The beer. _____

Six Days on the Road

Registration 4
Rhythm: Country or Fox Trot

Words and Music by Earl Green
and Carl Montgomery

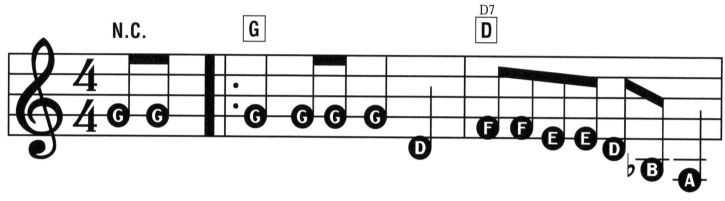

1. Well, I pulled out of Pitts - burgh, roll - in' down the East - ern Sea - ver -
ten for - ward gears and a Geor - gia o - ver -
3.-5. *(See additional lyrics)*

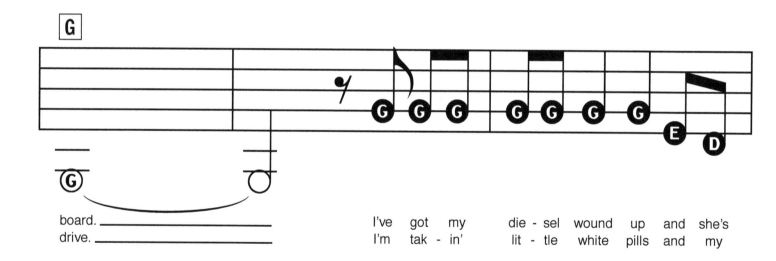

board. _____
drive. _____

I've got my die - sel wound up and she's
I'm tak - in' lit - tle white pills and my

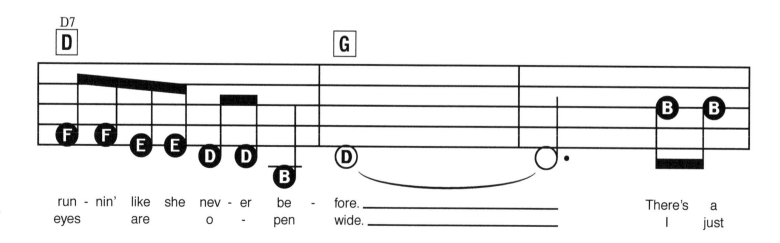

run - nin' like she nev - er be - fore. _____
eyes are o - pen wide. _____

There's a
I just

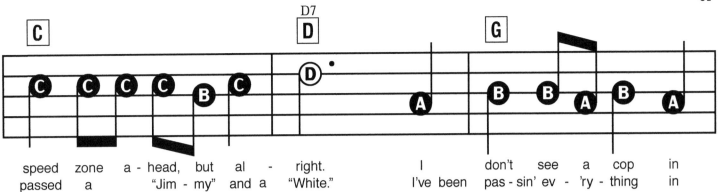

speed zone a - head, but al - right.
passed a "Jim - my" and a "White."

I

I don't see a cop in
I've been pas - sin' ev - 'ry - thing in

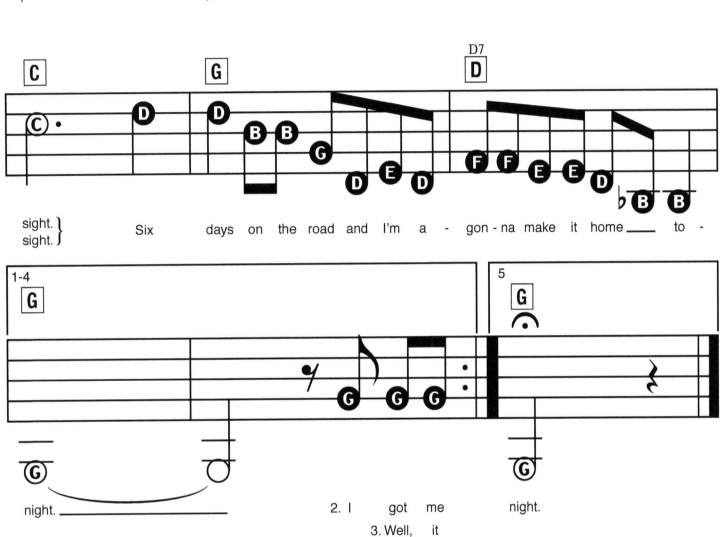

sight. } Six days on the road and I'm a - gon - na make it home ___ to -
sight. }

night. ___

2. I got me night.
3. Well, it

Additional Lyrics

3. Well, it seems like a month since I kissed my baby goodbye.
I could have a lot of women, but I'm not like some of the guys.
I could find one to hold me tight, but I could never make believe it's alright.
Six days on the road and I'm a-gonna make it home tonight.

4. Well, the I.C.C. is checkin' on down the line.
I'm a little overweight and my log book's way behind.
But nothing bothers me tonight, I can dodge all the scales alright.
Six days on the road and I'm a-gonna make it home tonight.

5. Well, my rig's a little old, but that don't mean she's slow.
There's a flame from her stack, and that smoke's blowin' black as coal.
My home town's comin' in sight: If you think I'm happy, you're right.
Six days on the road and I'm a-gonna make it home tonight.

Take This Job and Shove It

Registration 4
Rhythm: Country or Swing

Words and Music by
David Allen Coe

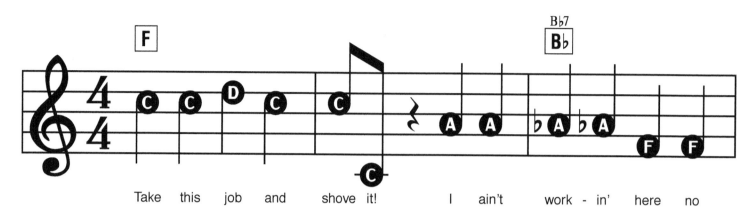

Take this job and shove it! I ain't work-in' here no

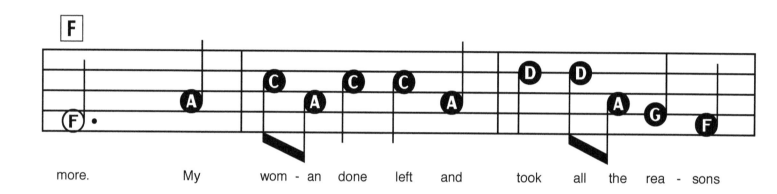

more. My wom-an done left and took all the rea-sons

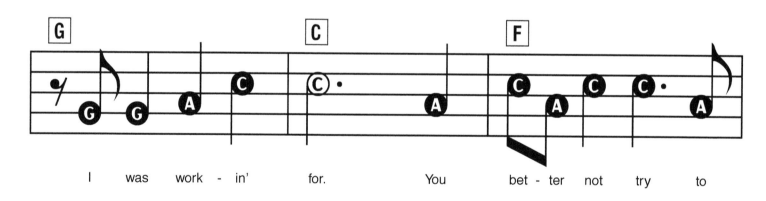

I was work-in' for. You bet-ter not try to

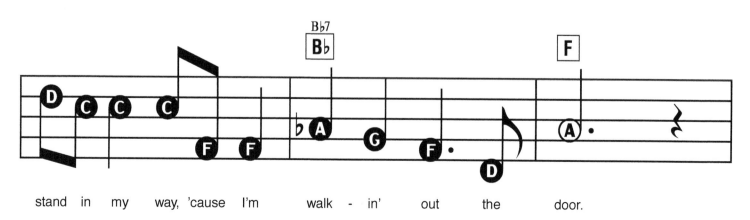

stand in my way, 'cause I'm walk-in' out the door.

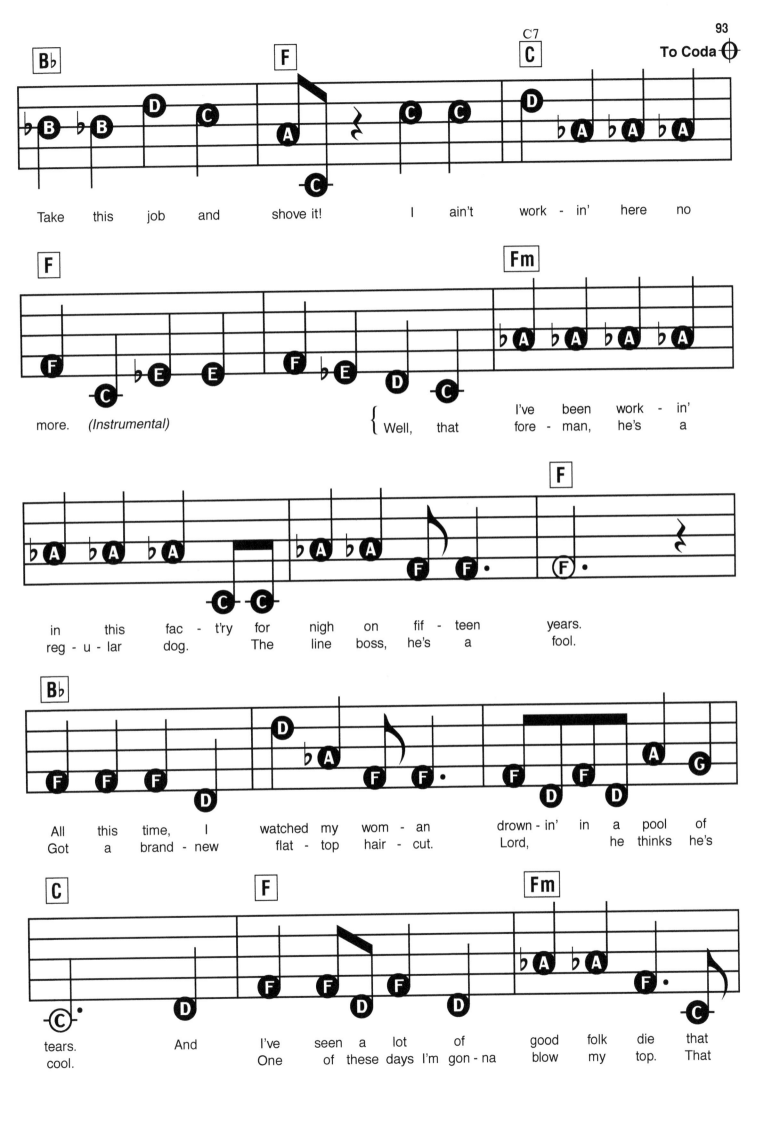

94

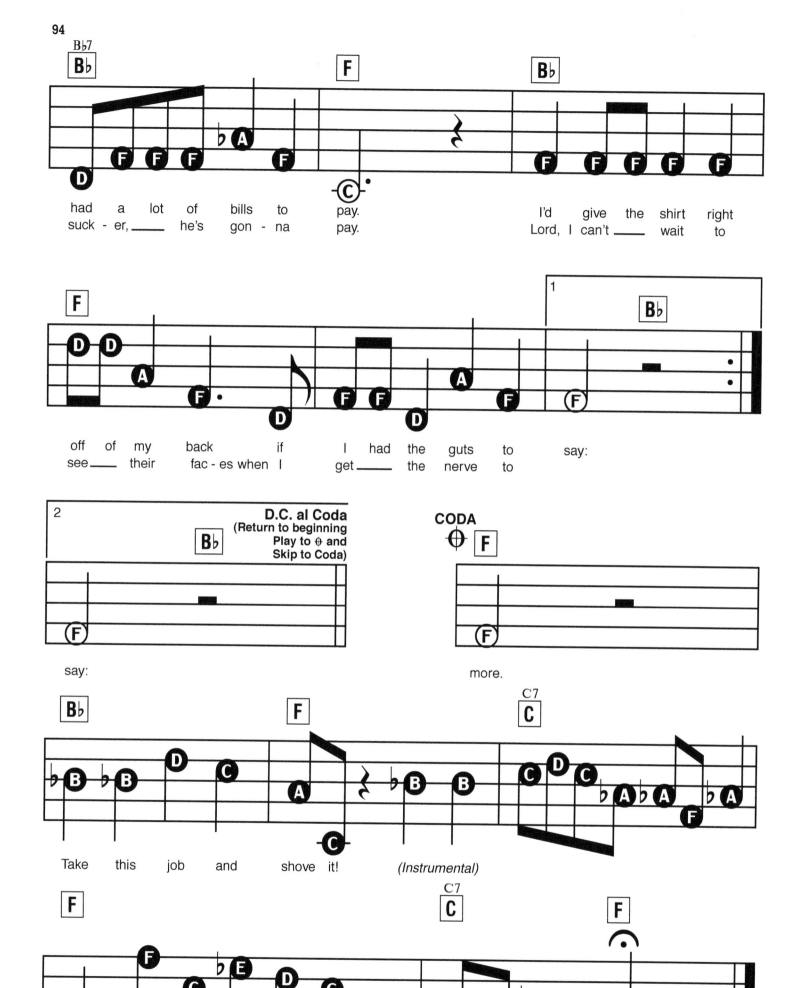

T for Texas

Registration 4
Rhythm: Country or Country Swing

Words and Music by
Jimmie Rodgers

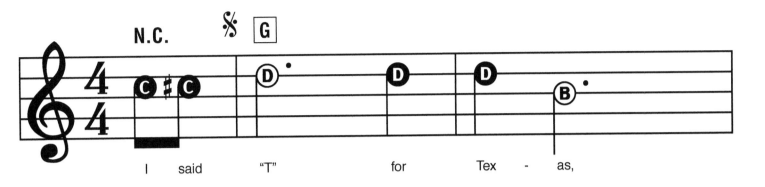

I said "T" for Tex - as,

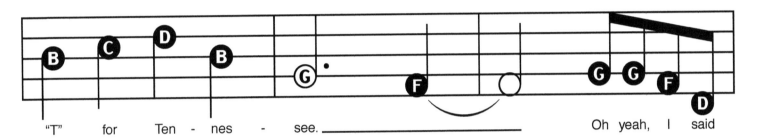

"T" for Ten - nes - see. _____ Oh yeah, I said

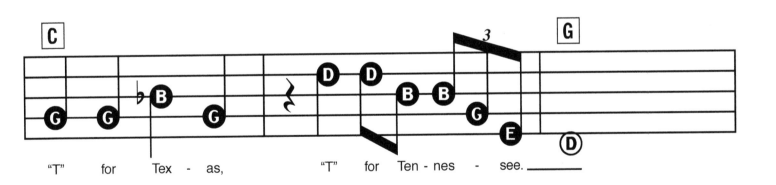

"T" for Tex - as, "T" for Ten - nes - see. _____

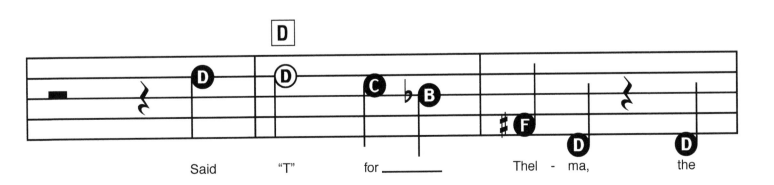

Said "T" for _____ Thel - ma, the

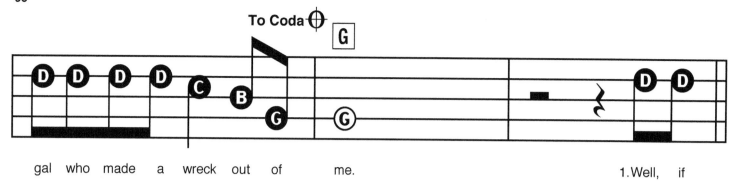

gal who made a wreck out of me.   1. Well, if

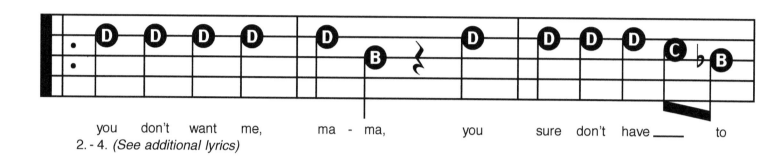

you don't want me, ma - ma, you sure don't have ___ to

2. - 4. *(See additional lyrics)*

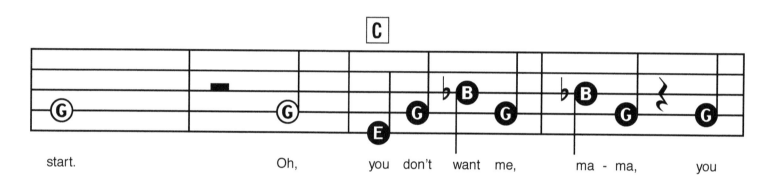

start.   Oh, you don't want me, ma - ma, you

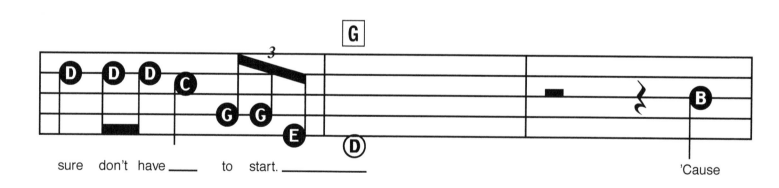

sure don't have ___ to start. ___   'Cause

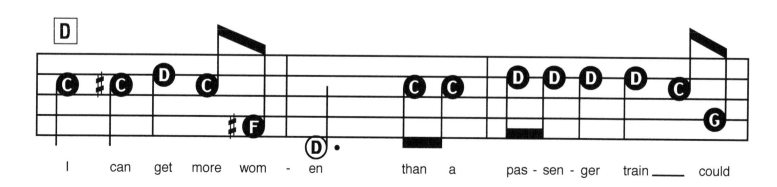

I can get more wom - en than a pas - sen - ger train ___ could

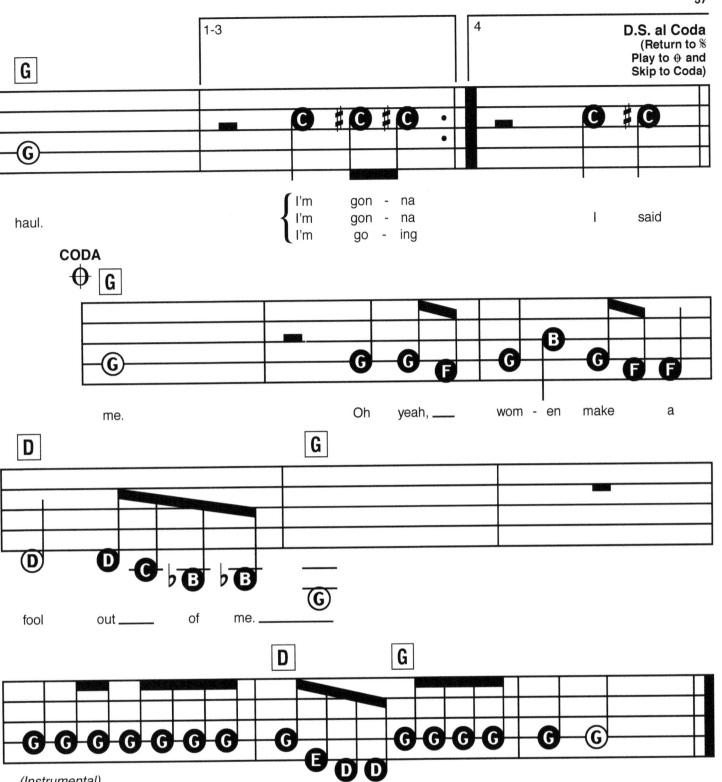

(Instrumental)

Additional Lyrics

2. I'm gonna buy me a pistol,
   Just as long as I am tall.
   I'm gonna buy me a pistol,
   Just as long as I am tall.
   I'm gonna shoot down old, mean Thelma
   Just to watch her jump and fall.

3. I'm gonna buy me a shotgun
   With a great, long, shiny barrel.
   I'm gonna buy me a shotgun
   With a great, long, shiny barrel.
   Gonna shoot down that rounder
   That stole my girl.

4. I'm going where the water
   Tastes like cherry wine.
   I'm going where the water
   Tastes like cherry wine,
   'Cause the water down here in Georgia
   Tastes like turpentine.

Two More Bottles of Wine

Registration 4
Rhythm: Country Rock

Words and Music by
Delbert McClinton

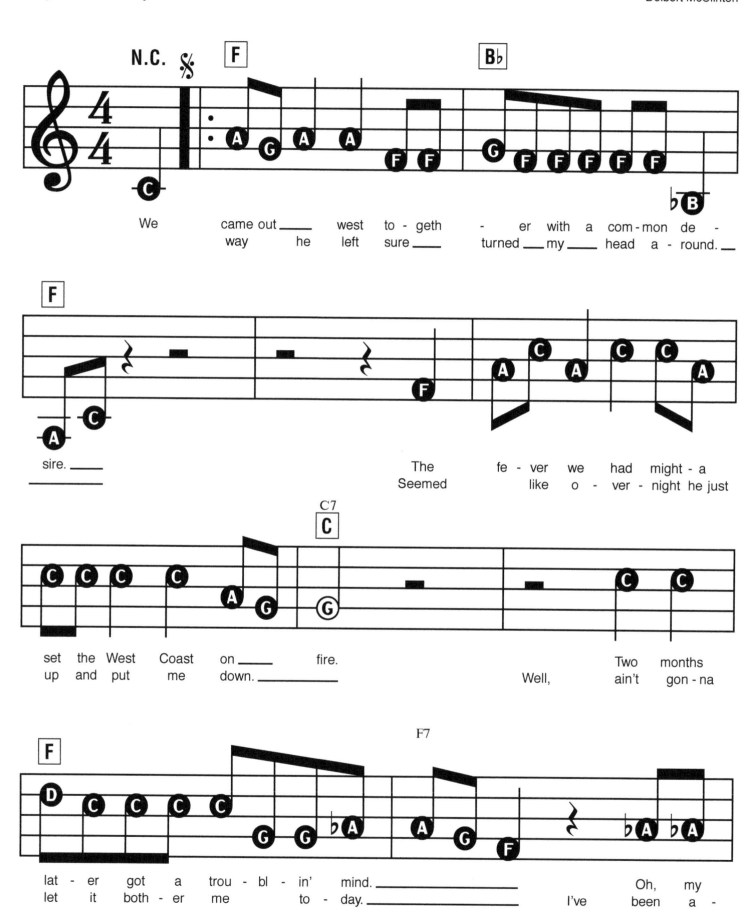

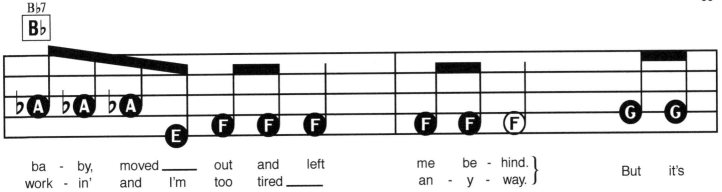

ba - by, moved ___ out and left me be - hind.
work - in' and I'm too tired ___ an - y - way.

But it's

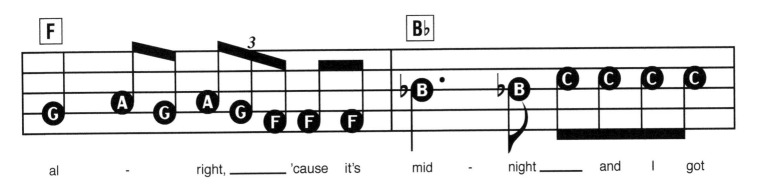

al - right, ___ 'cause it's mid - night ___ and I got

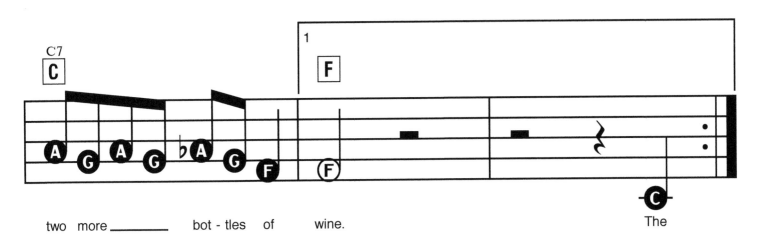

two more ___ bot - tles of wine.

The

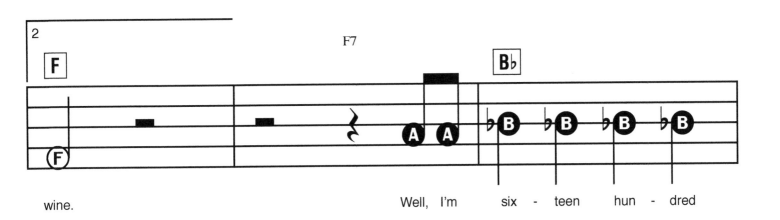

wine.

Well, I'm six - teen hun - dred

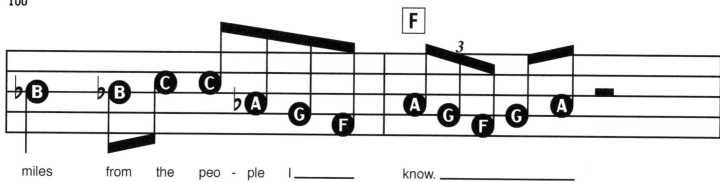

miles   from   the   peo - ple   I _____   know. _____

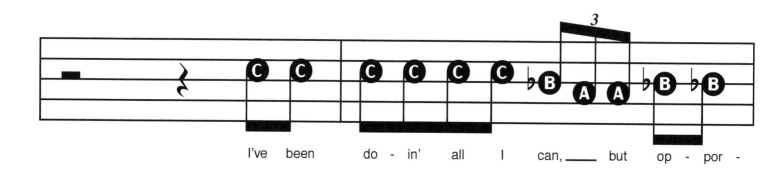

I've been   do - in'   all   I   can, ___ but   op - por -

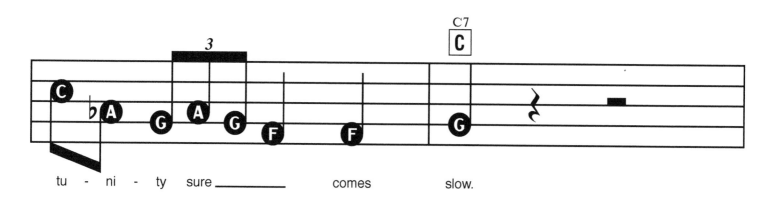

tu - ni - ty   sure _____   comes   slow.

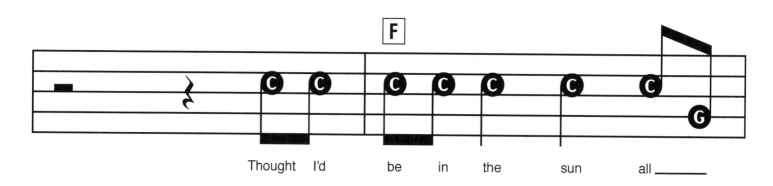

Thought   I'd   be   in   the   sun   all _____

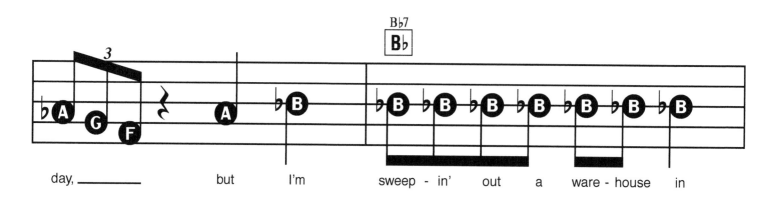

day, _____   but   I'm   sweep - in'   out   a   ware - house   in

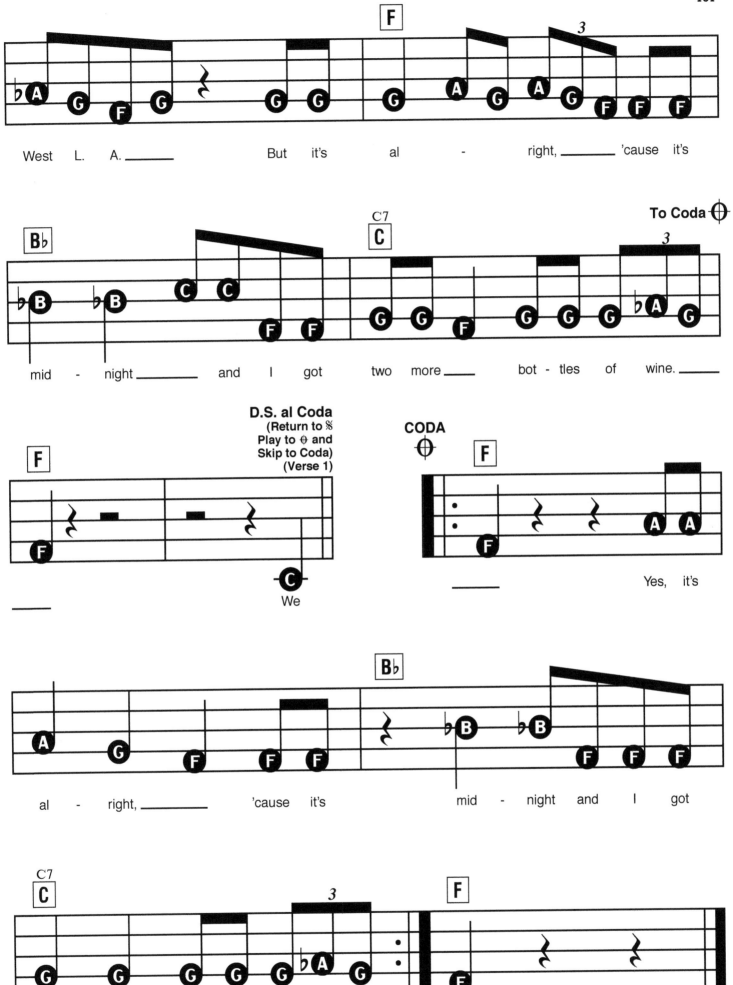

White Lightning

Registration 4
Rhythm: Country Rock

Words and Music by
J.P. Richardson

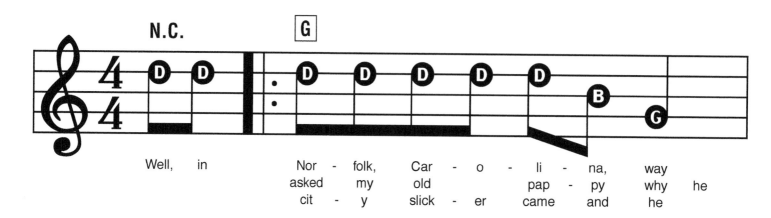

Well, in
Nor - folk, Car - o - li - na, way
asked my old pap - py why he
cit - y slick - er came and why he

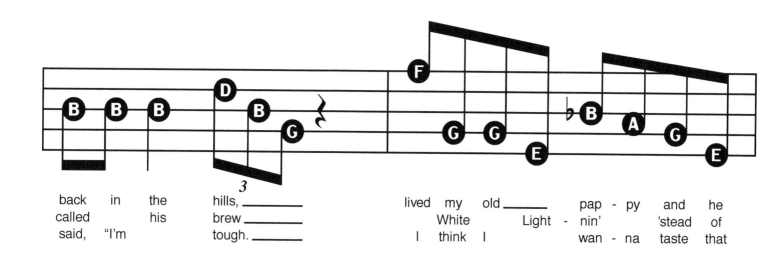

back in the hills, _____ lived my old _____ pap - py and he
called his brew _____ White Light - nin' 'stead of
said, "I'm tough. _____ I think I wan - na taste that

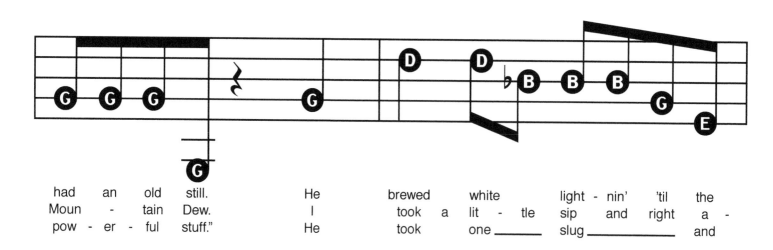

had an old still. He brewed white light - nin' 'til the
Moun - tain Dew. I took a lit - tle sip and right a -
pow - er - ful stuff." He took one _____ slug _____ and

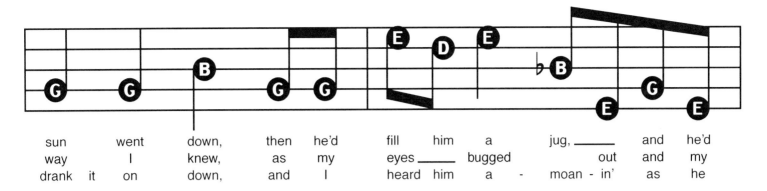

sun went down, then he'd fill him a jug, _____ and he'd
way I knew, as my eyes_____ bugged out and my
drank it on down, and I heard him a - moan - in' as he

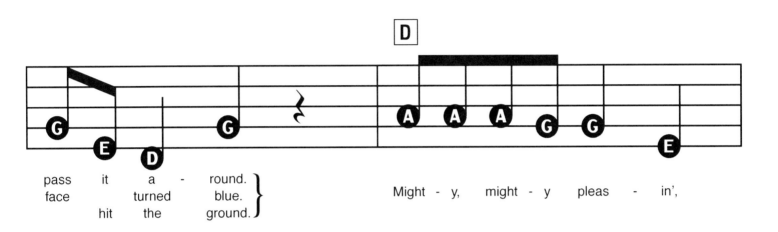

pass it a - round.
face turned blue.
hit the ground.

Might - y, might - y pleas - in',

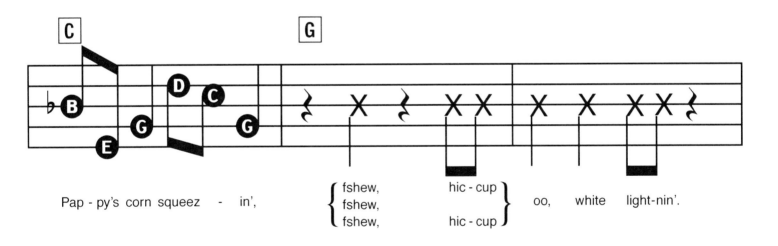

Pap - py's corn squeez - in',

fshew, hic - cup
fshew, hic - cup
fshew, hic - cup

oo, white light-nin'.

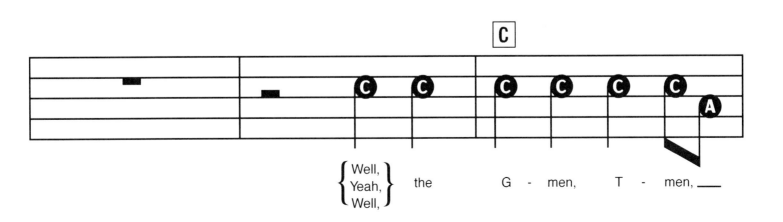

Well,
Yeah,
Well,

the G - men, T - men, ___

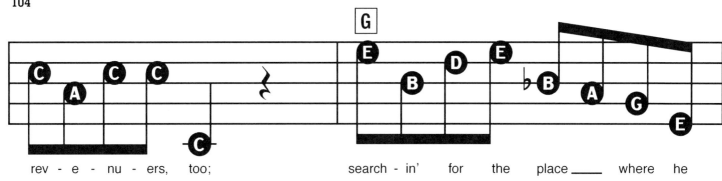

rev - e - nu - ers, too; search - in' for the place _____ where he

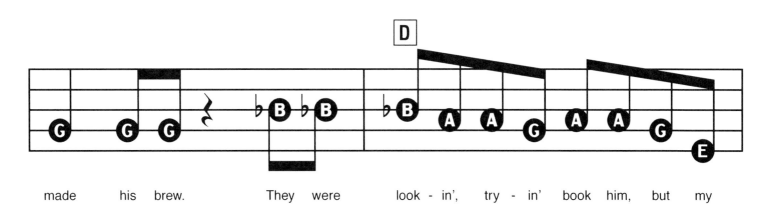

made his brew. They were look - in', try - in' book him, but my

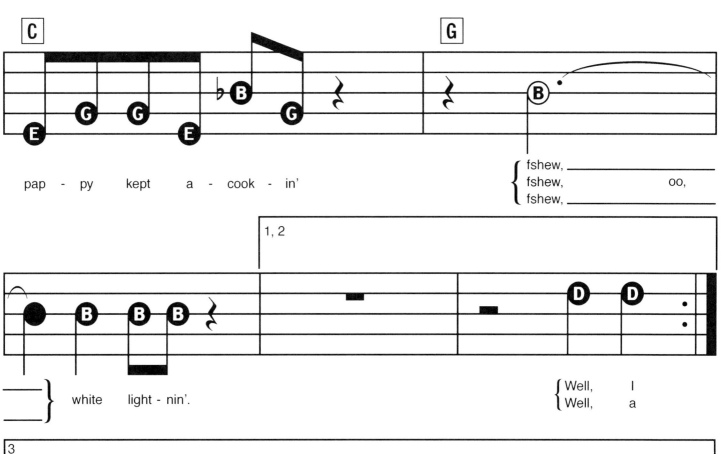

pap - py kept a - cook - in'

{ fshew, _____
{ fshew,   oo,
{ fshew, _____

1, 2

white light - nin'.

{ Well,   I
{ Well,   a

3

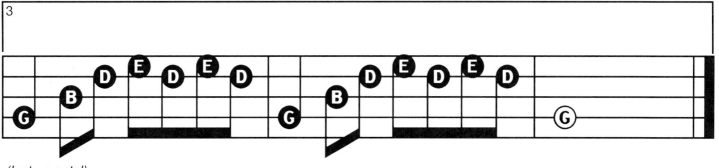

(Instrumental)